Suddenly
OVERBOARD

Suddenly OVERBOARD

True Stories of Sailors in Fatal Trouble

Tom Lochhaas

INTERNATIONAL MARINE/McGRAW-HILL EDUCATION

Camden, Maine | New York | Chicago | San Francisco | Athens | London
Madrid | Mexico City | Milan | New Delhi | Singapore | Sydney | Toronto

1 2 3 4 5 6 7 8 9 10 QFR/QFR 1 0 9 8 7 6 5 4 3

ISBN   978-0-07180331-1
MHID   0-07-180331-9

e-ISBN 978-0-07-180332-8
e-MHID   0-07-180332-7

Library of Congress Cataloging-in-Publication Data

Lochhaas, Thomas A.
      Suddenly overboard: true stories of sailors in fatal trouble / Tom Lochhaas.
          p.   cm.
      ISBN: 978-0-07-180331-1
      1. Sailors.   2. Seafaring life.   3. Boating accidents.   I. Title.

      G540.L76   2013
      910.4'5—dc23   2012043629

International Marine/McGraw-Hill Education products are available at special quantity
discounts to use as premiums and sales promotions or for use in corporate training
programs. To contact a representative, please e-mail us at bulksales@mcgraw-hill.com.

This book is printed on acid-free paper.

CONTENTS

Preface ix

Acknowledgments xiv

Introduction xv

Note on Imperial vs. Metric Units xxi

CHAPTER 1 | *The Storms We All Fear*
Chichester Bar | WingNuts | *Rally Boat to Bermuda* | *Briefly*
1

CHAPTER 2 | *Some Incidents Can't Be Prevented?*
Tangled in Rigging | *Lost Keel* | *Keep Treading!* | *The Tether Issue—An Opinion*
19

CHAPTER 3 | *A Good Day's Sail Goes Bad*
Just One Little Mistake | *Too Much Freeboard* | *Briefly*
35

CHAPTER 4 | *Anchoring, Docking, Dinghying*
Long Voyage, Quiet Harbor | *Late to the Slip* | *The Season's Last Sail* | *Briefly*
57

CHAPTER 5 | *Run Aground*
Tidal Estuary | *On the Rocks* | *The Reef of New South Wales* | *Briefly*
69

CHAPTER 6 | *Engine or Equipment Failure*
The Delivery Skipper | Take It Easy | *Briefly*
85

CHAPTER 7 | *A Gust of Wind*
Three Generations Sailing off Puffin Island | *A Hobie
on the Lake* | *Briefly*
99

CHAPTER 8 | *No Way to Call for Help*
Voices | *Short Sail on the Sound* | *The Inverted Cat* | *Briefly*
113

CHAPTER 9 | *A Thousand Ways to End Up in the Water*
To Save a Puppy | *Gone Fishing* | *Briefly*
129

CHAPTER 10 | *The Perils of Solo Sailing*
A Sailboat Comes Ashore | *The Fouled Halyard* | *Briefly*
141

CHAPTER 11 | *Can Your Crew Save You?*
Saturday on Lake Arthur | *Wednesday Evening
Club Race* | *Four Miles off Hyannis* | *Briefly*
153

CHAPTER 12 | *What Could Possibly Go Wrong?*
Capsize in Puget Sound | *Capsize in Lake Huron* | *Sinking
in the Georgia Strait* | *Bahia Transat Disaster*
169

Appendix | *Interview with Gary Jobson,
President of U.S. Sailing*
183

PREFACE

Twenty years ago I almost became a statistic. Although I'd sailed for a decade, had taken a boating safety course, and always took precautions like putting on my PFD (personal flotation device) when the wind or waves got up, I made one of those dumb mistakes everyone makes from time to time—if you're human. I can't imagine a stupider way to die.

It was a calm, beautiful day at the end of the season, and we were returning to the dock after a pleasant afternoon sail when it happened. At the time I was mostly just embarrassed. Afterward, with self-deprecating irony, I told it as a funny story. Years later, I learned it's one of the more common ways that sailors die on the water. Who'd have thought?

I kind of doubt my wife or daughter would've told it as a funny story if it had ended as so many real stories do.

In early October the waters of the Atlantic Ocean off New England—never warm—had already grown colder still. My friend Dan and I wore light jackets and jeans and socks under boat shoes, but the sun was warm and bright. My home port is a river harbor, just upstream from open ocean, and the tidal current can run 3 to 4 knots at half tide. We were used to that, of course, and factored it into our navigation. Trickier were the unpredictable eddies and side currents nearer shore and among the floating docks where I had a slip that summer for my 26-foot sloop. Still, not *that* tricky, and I was very accustomed to docking by myself after single-handed sailing. With crew, a piece of cake! Something I didn't even have to think about anymore.

Not thinking was my first mistake.

It was easy to motor into the slip slowly against the current, as I had so often before. Dan stepped off the port side with the bow line and walked forward to a cleat. I casually moved up to the port rail and stepped off with a stern line—and inexplicably found myself in the water.

I don't even remember how it happened. Later, Dan told me I'd been looking at him and pointing at which dock cleat to use when an eddy kicked the stern to starboard. I must have looked hilarious as I simply stepped over the rail and into the water.

I was right there beside the floating dock and easily held on, but damn was it cold! Fortunately the eddy kept the boat a few feet behind me rather than crushing me against the dock, but I wasn't thinking about the boat just then. I was wondering why in the world I couldn't pull myself up onto the dock. I grasped a cleat at the edge, but I had no leverage and couldn't brace my feet or legs against anything to climb up. The current swept my legs out at an angle, and already I was starting to shake with cold.

Dan cleated off the bow line, decided not to worry about keeping the boat from banging into the one to starboard, and came back to see if I needed a hand. When he saw I was apparently okay, he finally laughed. He grabbed one of my hands to help me out, but I was 200 pounds of dead weight, heavier still with my water-logged clothes, and he's a smaller guy. With a heave he yanked me high enough that I should have been able to hook a knee up on the float . . . but my legs seemed to have stopped working.

At this point in the story I usually let go with a string of epithets. In reality, I doubt I said much; the research shows panicking people, like those drowning, seldom actually call out for help, much less curse.

So there we were, me still wondering why I wasn't yet out of the water, Dan no doubt wondering that too—just climb out for God's sake! He still held one of my arms, but I couldn't feel the cleat anymore that my other hand clutched. My thinking was getting muddled and I considered letting go and letting the current drift me downstream where I was sure I'd bang up against the next dock where surely there was a ladder. Or whatever.

Maybe Dan saw the confusion in my eyes, or maybe he imagined having to tell my wife how he'd been unable to pull me out and could only watch helplessly as I slipped and went under, but abruptly he grabbed my other hand, locked tight on both wrists, crouched down, and with a mighty heave swung his weight backward and scraped my chest up onto the float like landing a giant fish that has died on the hook.

I just lay there shaking while he jerked me farther up a couple inches at a time. Eventually he grabbed my jeans above the knee and pulled my leg up on the float while I, somewhat mystified, noted that the heavy wet thing lying there was part of me.

I don't remember much about how he got the boat tied up and walked me to the car and got the heater running on high. I just remember being really cold and looking down at my numb hands that felt like blocks of wood attached to my arms. I have to be honest here: as scared as I should've been, I don't think it occurred to me that I actually—really, truly—could have died in such a dumb way. I know that because, even with the benefit of that experience, I didn't immediately start doing things differently. Well, sure, I was more careful jumping onto docks. I learned that old lesson to look before you leap—and look again. But I didn't start wearing my PFD religiously, at all times and in all places, for years. It had just been a fluke, right?

That was almost 20 years ago. In subsequent years I moved up to larger and larger cruising sailboats, wrote articles for sailing magazines and a couple of books, and researched safety gear ad nauseum for a voyage I was then planning across the Atlantic. I helped write a boating safety book published by the American Red Cross and Coast Guard Auxiliary. I made a few offshore voyages from New England to the Caribbean and back. I thought I'd learned about most things that could happen in a storm at sea, and made long lists of equipment to have on board to prevent or manage such disasters.

Then a few years ago, several incidents happened in my local area. A sailor who rowed out to his moored sailboat slipped off the boarding ladder and drowned as the current swept him away within view of onlookers on shore. Another sailor moored his boat in the harbor after a day of sailing, slipped on some slimy seaweed that had dripped from his mooring pendant onto the foredeck, and went over the rail; unable to get back on the boat, he drowned. Another highly experienced sailor was stepping off his dinghy to board his boat at a local yacht club and went into the water, hidden from view by another boat, as his wife watched from shore. By the time she saw the dinghy drifting free and called for help, it was too late.

It had been years since any sailors died in a storm in New England, but then three died on calm days in harbor where we all usually feel safe. If that much was happening in my tiny sliver of New England waters, how many such incidents were occurring nationally or worldwide? Why hadn't I heard more about such accidents?

I started analyzing Coast Guard reports of sailing fatalities. The published statistics don't actually tell us much; of course most boaters die from drowning, but what actually led to that? It was possible to find the actual stories online, however, and not just sailing deaths in the United States but all around the world. Every harbor town, every lake, every coast. The more I read—hundreds and hundreds of narratives of sailing fatalities, near fatalities, and lucky rescues—the more shocked I became. There were hundreds of ways to die! And the huge majority of them came from simple, everyday occurrences, not storms at sea or fires aboard or hitting a submerged object in the water and sinking the boat, all those things we've been taught to fear and try to prepare for. All those bestselling books about perfect storms and dramatic sea disasters seemed to have misdirected our fears (and safety precautions) off in only one or two directions, while meanwhile the grim reaper kept appearing in scores of other guises.

I'm not shocked anymore by all this information. Now I'm horrified.

Horrified, first, to realize that experienced, competent sailors do die just as I almost did, stepping off their boat onto a dock. Horrified to read so many other stories of sailors doing everyday things, just as I always had, that led to fatal consequences.

Horrified to realize that I had been at the edge of that cliff in the dark so many times, and that if I kept on sailing for another 30 years, the odds might slowly turn against me.

And horrified too to see so many other sailors making the same mistakes or taking the same risks, and almost always at times they thought there was no risk at all.

When there is a fatal disaster in a big yacht club race or other dramatic situation, it usually gets lots of press. Commissions are formed to investigate what went wrong. Recommendations are issued. Equipment is mandated. Many dollars are spent. But when two kids sailing a Sunfish on a lake end up dead, it makes only the local newspaper. When someone falls overboard reaching for a puppy or a hat and dies, family and friends grieve, but no national safety bulletins are issued. The stories aren't talked about where sailors gather or in the glossy magazines. "Death by drowning" appears in the statistics, but other sailors seldom hear about the everyday circumstances behind them.

There may be hundreds of ways to die while sailing, but preventing the huge majority of them doesn't require expensive safety gear, reports from commissions, or elaborate training programs.

It just requires knowing how it happens. And thinking and talking about it—an attitude adjustment of sorts.

My own attitude changed as I read more and more of the real stories. And I'm sailing more than ever now, happier than ever—and safer than ever.

Hopefully, reading these stories may have the same benefits for you.

ACKNOWLEDGMENTS

'd like to thank the following organizations and individuals for providing source material for the narratives in this book.

- The United States Coast Guard, which provides a wealth of boating safety information on its websites along with annual accident and fatality reports, and which provided personal assistance with more detailed incident reports for all sailing fatalities in U.S. waters over the last 4 years.
- The Marine Accident Investigation Branch of the United Kingdom, which provides similar detailed information and reports about all significant boating incidents in UK waters.
- U.S. Sailing, which investigates and reports on significant incidents that occur during sailboat races.
- The Canadian Coast Guard, which provides statistical reports and information similar to that of its American counterpart.
- State agencies that provided me with more specific information about sailing incidents that led to recent fatalities: California Department of Boating and Waterways, Connecticut Department of Energy and Environmental Protection, Michigan Department of Natural Resources, Oregon State Marine Board, Pennsylvania Fish and Boat Commission, and Washington State Parks and Recreation Commission.
- The many dozens of journalists of local and regional newspapers who have made the effort to uncover and report enough detail about boating incidents so that we can learn from what happened.

And most especially, thanks to all the coast guard and life-saving organizations around the globe who conduct search-and-rescue missions and to their brave men and women who risk their own lives to rescue sailors who find themselves in trouble.

INTRODUCTION

*S*uddenly Overboard is about sailing emergencies we don't usually hear about. Aside from a few storm stories included to round out the representative spectrum of things that can go wrong when sailing, you won't find the dramas of storms or sail races where a dozen boats capsize here. Those are the big stories, the ones that make the news and become movies, the stories that have led generations of sailors to presume that storms are what we have most to fear and prepare for. Hence the multimillion-dollar industry of must-have sailboat equipment and the library of books on heavy-weather sailing. This is not to minimize the threat of storms at sea or the precautions we sailors should take, but it belies the reality that the huge majority of sailing-related fatalities and rescues have nothing to do with storms.

Most of the stories here, in contrast, involve circumstances less grand and cinematic. Often the water is calm. Adrenaline is not flowing. Usually things happen quickly and unexpectedly, not after hours or days of "sailor against the sea." Almost always the victims or survivors are enjoying their time on the water just before disaster strikes.

But this doesn't mean their stories are any less dramatic or emotional than the classic storm-battling incidents we've all learned about. Any incident involving a confrontation with mortality holds human drama—too often, tragedy—and demands our respect. And we learn from them just the same, or perhaps more so, since few of us will confront great storms, while everyone who gets on a boat, dinghy or cruiser, on a lake or an ocean, is every time in the same circumstances as the sailors in these stories.

Sources of the Stories

All the stories included here are true and have been documented. In the United States, the Coast Guard maintains records for all boating fatalities and reports on most rescue attempts. Equivalent agencies in Canada, the United Kingdom, Australia, and New Zealand do the same, often conducting extensive investigations. Other groups such as sailing associations also frequently investigate fatalities. Sometimes, as in a dramatic storm or race disaster, these are reported in sailing magazines and the popular press, these being the stories sailors *do* hear about. But for every disaster that makes headlines, like the *WingNuts* fatal capsize in a 2011 race (see Chapter 1), there are literally hundreds of other sailing disasters we seldom hear about.

I discovered that these stories too can be found when you go looking. Small-town newspapers post online stories of local incidents that can be searched out. Boating fatalities in the United States are required to be reported to state agencies, typically law enforcement, that then provide reports to the U.S. Coast Guard to be included in national statistics. Such statistics often do not include much detail about what actually happened in the series of events that resulted in a "death by drowning." To understand—and learn from—the original causes and other factors involved, we need the details from witnesses at the scene, investigators, and journalists.

With an average of about 700 boating fatalities in the United States every year, and hundreds more reported in English-speaking areas around the world, that's a lot of stories. Add to this the literally thousands of incidents of rescues and injuries and near fatalities every year. Fortunately for sailors, sailboats are involved less frequently than other types of watercraft, yet there are still hundreds of incidents a year. Those stories, from all those sources, form the raw material for this book.

Again, these are all true stories, and I have recounted them as truly as I can. In some cases there were hundreds of pages of information related to a single incident. In some cases I've spoken to survivors or others with knowledge of the incident. But in other cases, such as when a solo sailor went overboard without witnesses, I could tell the story only through what documentarians call "dramatic reconstruction," based as faithfully as possible on the facts but still, of necessity, partly speculative, based on my knowledge of similar events.

A final note on the sources and the retelling. Most U.S. and international government agencies attempt to preserve the anonymity of victims and survivors in their public reports. Names and specific identifying information are redacted. Not only does this respect the privacy of the individuals involved, but it also helps maintain a climate in which people are not hesitant to report details they might otherwise not want to share for fear of public embarrassment. In many cases, as I read those anonymous reports, I recognized the incidents and knew the names of the people involved, as printed in local news reports at the time. Nevertheless, this book follows the same principles of anonymity. A story is just as true without the person's name, and there is simply no compelling reason to include identifying information in these stories, except in a few cases already somewhat famous in the press and therefore identifiable. So most names and some other specifics of identity have been changed to maintain that anonymity.

What the Stories Show

While there are hundreds of incidents every year, there are not hundreds of conclusions to be drawn. The more stories I read, the simpler the "lesson" seemed to become.

First, a few statistics. While numbers are often ultimately less convincing than experiences, they provide an interesting and useful backdrop for the stories.

Here's a quick overview of the most recent year's statistics available from the U.S. Coast Guard. Of all fatalities involving sailboats, the cause of death in 83% of cases was drowning. That number is even higher if hypothermia caused by water immersion is included. No surprises here; water is not the normal human environment, and our bodies are ill equipped for unplanned immersion in deep water. Nor is it greatly surprising that in 89% of sailing fatalities by drowning, the victim was not wearing a PFD. And in all sailboat incidents, the most common contributing factor was classified as "operator inattention."

This much is perhaps obvious—if you end up in the water without a PFD, you're at risk for drowning—but it doesn't tell us much about *how* the victims ended up in the water and *why* they weren't wearing a PFD.

For a start in that direction, we can look at other Coast Guard studies and surveys of boater behavior. Now it gets more interesting. Only 22% of adults in all sailboats say they wear a PFD all or most of the time. The rate is higher for those in small daysailers but is only 12% for sailors in cabin sailboats. Further, despite many boating safety campaigns and other efforts to increase the use of PFDs (including emphasis on more comfortable and less bulky inflatable types), in the 12 years since the Coast Guard started these studies, the percentage of boaters wearing PFDs has actually decreased.

Data comparing sailors with other classifications of boaters adds an interesting dimension to this picture. A higher percentage of sailors (over 62%), compared to other classes of boaters, have taken a boating safety course. So why then are sailors less likely to wear a PFD? Another interesting statistic is that a higher percentage of sailors know how to swim than other groups of boaters. Could overconfidence when on the water be a factor here?

Just a few more numbers. Regarding what victims were actually doing with the sailboat at the time of an incident that resulted in a fatality, *only about 50% were actually sailing*. The other half were at anchor, docking, motoring in the harbor, swimming off the boat, etc. Again, these are times when many people might not be wearing a PFD because they didn't perceive they were in a risky situation.

Finally, I developed my own analysis of the circumstances of sailors in the water, based on all reported fatalities over the last 4 years. Only about 25% of victims were in the water because the boat had capsized, mostly small daysailers you'd expect might capsize in a gust and therefore should be prepared for. In another 15% of cases, the person was deliberately in the water, swimming or for another reason. And in a perhaps astonishing 40% of cases, sailors drowned with the boat still upright and usually nearby after unexpectedly, for a variety of reasons, ending up in the water.

Okay, that's lots of numbers, and still they don't really show *exactly why* most fatalities occur. What they do demonstrate, however, is that *the most dangerous time for sailors is the least dangerous time.* That is, the sailors about to become victims perceived no significant danger or risk at the time. Life was going well, the sailing was good, it was just another day on the water. In perhaps only 5% of cases would the sailor about to die have said he or she felt any danger.

What Sailors Can Do About It

The Coast Guard and every boating safety course urge all boaters to wear PFDs at all times, and obviously this would make a huge difference in the fatality statistics. But as we've already seen, saying it doesn't make it so, and that change alone still would not completely solve the problem and ensure sailors' safety.

My own view is that staying safe on a sailboat begins with an attitude of thinking ahead about anything that can happen at any time on the water. Again, this means not just simply being ready for storms and having lots of gear on the boat for emergencies, and not just the traditional seamanship skills of navigation and boat operation, but always thinking ahead and asking yourself "what if" this or that happens right now. If you know the odds are greater that you'll die after falling overboard on a calm day in the goofiest of circumstances (and you'll know that after reading these stories), then you're more likely to wear your PFD and take other actions in such circumstances.

Unfortunately, it's hard to teach an attitude in a boating safety course. And you won't read much about it in the safety or seamanship chapters of most sailing books, which often focus on skills and equipment and emergency preparations. Indeed, in a survey of dozens of such books I found only one expert directly confronting this issue of attitude and how it may be formed. Don Dodds, in *Modern Seamanship*, a now-out-of-print 1995 book, wrote the following in his introduction to a chapter on common emergencies:

> *[Most] accidents are the result of bad planning, poor judgment, or failing to think. Not much can be done about poor judgment, but something can be done about bad planning and failing to think. . . . Talk is cheap, consumes little time, and attracts little attention. Take a little time to talk about fire on board, people lost overboard, and other common emergencies. It can be done at lunch, over a cocktail, or anytime the crew is gathered and there is a lull in activity. Detailed discussion will encourage each crewmember to think about emergency procedures ahead of time. Thinking fast is a myth. Show me a person who thinks fast and I'll show you a person who has thought the situation through beforehand.*

Exactly! Now all we need to know is what those "common emergencies" really are so we can think and talk about what to do if they occur. A fire extinguisher is important, yes, but fires account for less than 1% of sailboat incidents; *what else* should we be talking about?

In short, what accounts for the 99% of disasters? What *really* happens out there on the water that leads to so many incidents and deaths?

Read the stories.

NOTE ON
IMPERIAL VS. METRIC UNITS

This book includes stories from around the world, most of which include descriptions of measurements such as boat length and weight, water and air temperatures, distance, and so on. Including both imperial and metric units for each measurement would in many cases have introduced errors because of customary rounding. For example, in the United States a 26-foot boat may in reality be 25 feet and 8 inches or even 26 feet and 2 inches, yet it is still referred to as a 26-foot boat. To add its metric length (7.9 meters for 26 feet) could therefore be incorrect, as the number 7.9 implies a level of precision that may simply be false. In the United Kingdom this boat may or may not be referred to as an 8-meter boat. Yet to refer to it as a "26-foot (8-meter) boat" would be mathematically incorrect.

For this reason, and to avoid the intrusiveness of giving two numbers in every instance, the units used in these stories are those mentioned in the source materials, whether from Coast Guard and Marine Accident Investigation Branch reports or journalists' accounts.

Following are standard (approximate) conversions between imperial and metric units appearing in this book:

1 foot = 0.30 meters — 1 meter = 3.3 feet
Examples: a 14-foot boat = 4.3 meters
a 36-foot boat = 11 meters
a 6-meter boat = 19.7 feet

1 pound (lb) = 0.454 kilograms (kg) — 1 kg = 2.2 lb
Examples: a 4,000-lb boat = 1,814 kg
a 300-kg keel = 660 lb

Nautical miles (n.m.) are used for all distances on the water. Boat speeds are given in nautical miles per hour (knots).

1 n.m. = 1.15 miles = 1.85 kilometers (km)
Example: 120 n.m. = 138 miles = 222 km

Water and air temperatures in Fahrenheit (F) and Celsius (C) vary in part because 0°C (the freezing point) is 32°F. Each degree F is approximately 5/9 degree C, but the 32° must be added or subtracted when making the conversion.

Examples: 45° F = 7° C
60° F = 16° C
10° C = 50° F
26° C = 79° F

Wind speed is generally given in nautical miles per hour (knots) in the United States, and according to the Beaufort scale (Force) in the United Kingdom.

Force 1 = 1–3 knots = "light air"
Force 2 = 4–6 knots = "light breeze"
Force 3 = 7–10 knots = "gentle breeze"
Force 4 = 11–16 knots = "moderate breeze"
Force 5 = 17–21 knots = "fresh breeze"
Force 6 = 22–27 knots = "strong breeze"
Force 7 = 28–33 knots = "near gale"
Force 8 = 34–40 knots = "gale"
Force 9 = 41–47 knots = "strong gale"
Force 10 = 48–55 knots = "storm"
Force 11 = 56–63 knots = "violent storm"
Force 12 = 64–71 knots = "hurricane"

CHAPTER 1

The Storms
We All Fear

Storms: what sailors fear most, and what keep many from sailing offshore for fear of high winds and seas. With modern technology, forecasting, and better communication, however, few boats encounter hurricanes and typhoons, although even a passing thunderstorm or squall can still produce winds high enough to cause problems. Storms often pose a great threat for racers who may carry more sail, or attempt riskier maneuvers, or hesitate to heave-to or seek safe harbor, but even a cautious daysailor may encounter winds or waves high enough to threaten. A storm may threaten life by severely damaging the boat, although this is seldom the primary cause of storm fatalities. Most medium to large sailboats are built ruggedly enough to withstand a knockdown, and a prudent sailor has tactics such as heaving-to or using a sea anchor to prevent one. Even in the worst storms, it is most critical to stay on the boat and avoid injury from being battered by the storm's violence. In the worst-case scenarios, safety gear, such as a radio, an EPIRB (emergency position-indicating radio beacon), a life raft, and so on, greatly increases your odds for staying alive.

This is not to say there are no "acts of God," only that storms themselves are a relatively rare cause of death of sailors and that, as these stories show, in most cases preventive efforts are, or would have been, lifesaving.

Chichester Bar

From the moment they'd met, there was something about the guy that William didn't like. Generally easygoing, William put up with all sorts of boatowner personalities—it was just part of the job—but he'd have happily said no to Hank if it weren't so late in the season and delivery jobs weren't so scarce.

In his experience, there were two typical types of boatowners who hired delivery skippers: the ones who admitted they were too inexperienced to sail their boat on their own to some other location, and the rich ones who just wanted to pay someone to move their boats for them. The former often made good crew and were eager to learn, and William was happy enough to teach, while the latter stayed home or at the office as he, also happily enough, moved the boat with his own crew.

But this one, Hank, seemed conflicted and was arrogant to boot. He couldn't quite admit he needed help to sail his 8.5-meter sailboat from Chichester Harbour in the south of England to Dartmouth for a winter refit, roughly 120 nautical miles. He acted almost as if he was letting William come along for the short voyage as a favor. He was too bossy for William's taste. Well, he thought, as he signed the delivery contract after inspecting the boat, Hank also seemed the type to end up seasick down below, and William didn't mind sailing by himself, not at all.

It wasn't the best forecast, but perfect weather was rare in the UK in November. Today the wind was supposed to be 15 to 20 knots southwest, so they'd have to beat their way west through the Solent. Tomorrow it might get heavier, but they'd deal with that tomorrow. There were plenty of good harbors to duck into if it got nasty. "Any port in a storm," he'd said to Hank as they made plans, but the guy had only scowled as if to say *he* wasn't afraid of weather, come what may.

To top things off, Hank was late to their meeting so they missed the ebb when they left Chichester Harbour. It was late afternoon before they'd motored over the bar and made full sail, shutting off the noisy old diesel that Hank was having rebuilt in Dartmouth.

The beat through the Solent was much the same as always, something William could do with his eyes closed. The little sloop did a lot of crash-banging nonetheless, but he was happy enough to be underway, even in the chill of November as the sun dropped. And he was happy that Hank stayed huddled under the dodger and kept quiet while William took the helm.

"Ought to put on a life jacket," he'd advised Hank once, eliciting that arrogant scowl again. To which William made a show of clipping his tether to the binnacle, which he might not have done otherwise unless it got rough. But he always wore his PFD with a harness, which felt comfortable after years of wear. William had seen four or five life jackets and harnesses stowed below when he'd checked out the boat yesterday, but he preferred to bring his own.

Hank took the helm for a while before dark, when William tucked in a reef for the night and the building wind. William didn't care for how the man steered, however, heading up and falling off repeatedly, and soon reclaimed the helm.

At ten o'clock he put in another reef and turned on the radio for the hourly forecast. Didn't sound good: gales were imminent. Oddly, Hank didn't even look up from his place under the dodger during the forecast. It was as if he was going to force William to be the one to say anything, since he himself was a masterful enough sailor for anything.

"We have a couple options," William said at last. "It's pointless to beat into a gale all night and get nowhere. So I say we put in at Lymington or Yarmouth. Either harbor will get us through the night, and hopefully things will settle for a morning start."

In the dark Hank's eyes were barely visible as he stared out from the dodger, but he didn't speak.

"I'd vote for Yarmouth myself," William went on. "Better protected if the blow goes more southerly. But it's your boat, so you decide."

Hank hauled himself out from under the dodger into the full force of the wind for the first time in hours. He staggered as he stood and watched the flickering lightning off to the west. "No," he said slowly. "If you won't go on, let's go back to Chichester."

That made no sense to William. Why give up the 26 nautical miles they'd already made?

But Hank offered no good explanation, and William soon got tired of talking about it. Boatowners! As if this tired old sloop demanded its royal berth home in Chichester. But he gave in and set a return course on a broad reach back toward the east.

Gales tonight, he was thinking, but at least they were reaching now instead of beating. Still, he anticipated a long night. He left the two reefs in.

Only once more did he ask Hank to take the helm, when he went below for his foulies, and almost immediately he regretted it. The guy just couldn't steer! An accidental jibe seemed likely any moment under Hank's hand, and the shock of that—or of being rolled by a backwinded main if they tied in a preventer— might bring down the rig. And the guy still wouldn't put on a life jacket.

At 4 A.M. the radio reported steady 38-knot winds in the Solent and gusts approaching 50. Out here in deeper water the waves had built only to 2 meters and were full of curling white horses, but William was thinking ahead to the Chichester Bar. He checked the tide chart. "Looks like we won't make it before the ebb," he told Hank. "In this blow the bar will be breaking on the ebb, and I don't think we want to get caught in there. We'll have to stand off until the wind drops or until slack."

"We're almost home free," Hank growled. This time William couldn't see his eyes in the dark space under the dodger. "She's a good boat—we'll go on in."

They could wait for morning light, that would help some, William thought, but by then the ebb would reach its peak and it would be breaking heavily over the bar. "At least put on your life jacket and a tether," William said. He wanted it to sound like an order from the captain, but not so much so that it would antagonize the owner.

He was happy to see the other man go below then. But in a few minutes he came back out, still without a life jacket or harness. It had now started raining, and the water stung William's eyes whenever he glanced back at a following sea. With no protection from the dodger with the wind aft, Hank unrolled his jacket hood and covered most of his face.

William squinted to peer forward in the rain and dark at the Chichester Bar beacon ahead, trying to judge the waves. The depthfinder and his handheld GPS showed they were getting close. The seas were building, lifting the stern higher and slewing them sideways, but William was able to steer each wave as it passed, walking the delicate line between broaching to port and jibing to starboard.

Then a big wave struck just before they reached the bar, as the water heaved up over the rising sea bottom. When the stern began to lift he instinctively looked back over his shoulder, not even seeing the wave at first in the dark because its white curling top was so high—it had to be 6 meters. Before he could even think, it broke and slammed the port quarter with massive force, knocking the boat down to starboard and flooding the cockpit with water. He held on as best he could, but was knocked loose. He felt his harness tighten around his chest as his shorter tether went tight, and he threw one arm over his head for protection and closed his mouth and eyes against the water.

The boat must have been knocked right over 90 degrees, he realized later, because just before it rolled back up, he'd slipped and started to fall to his left but instead bumped his shoulder against the port cockpit seat vertical beside him.

Hank was gone, thrown or washed overboard. In the white foam of the departing wave William saw him for a second in the water, only some 7 or 8 meters behind, but the boat was quickly blown away from him. William grabbed the dan-buoy from its rail mount and threw it toward him but lost sight of the man in the water.

Acting automatically, William turned the boat hard to port to bring the bow up and released both sheets when the boat was as close to the wind as he could get it. In the turmoil of the waves breaking over the bar he'd never be able to reach Hank under sail. He turned the key and jabbed the starter button, barely able to hear the engine grinding in the roaring wind, but the engine would not catch. He tried again, tried everything he knew, then gave up and made a Mayday call on the radio.

As he gave his location and described the man in the water, the boat shook as it was slammed aground by a wave. It quickly rolled onto its side, driven into a groin in the shallows. William took a few seconds to get his bearings—to calculate the water depth and the waves and the distance to shore—and then unclipped his tether, yanked the cord to inflate his PFD, and jumped overboard.

It took a long time to scramble up on the shore, and he lay on the beach panting as the first rescue boat roared out of the harbor headed for the bar.

Soon he heard a helicopter.

They found Hank's body an hour later.

WingNuts

At age 51, Mark had been sailing his whole life along with his younger brother, Peter. As kids they raced small sailboats on lakes, graduating to larger boats and races on Lake Michigan and elsewhere. No question, they were highly capable sailors. Previous to the 2011 Race to Mackinac, Mark had done the two-day Chicago–Mac five times and Peter four, along with dozens of other races. Suzanne, Mark's girlfriend, and one of the crew this year, was doing her third Chicago–Mac and had also sailed across the Atlantic. When you looked at their credentials they seemed like professional racers, but they held jobs in the "real world." Still, they seemed sailors first, and were skilled, able competitors.

Mark and Peter were also members of a close-knit extended family. With cousins John and Stanton, they'd purchased *Wing-Nuts*, their current entry in the race, and they sailed it together, along with Peter's son. In photos they looked like a poster family for club racing.

They were excited for another Chicago–Mac and had hopes of winning the sport-boat class.

Held by the Chicago Yacht Club, the Chicago–Mac has been an annual event for a century, making it one of the oldest organized races in the United States. Well over 300 sailboats usually compete, with 345 registered in 2011. Lake Michigan, the race site, is scarcely a "lake" in any sense of that word except for being fresh water. Conditions on the 333–nautical mile course across the length of Lake Michigan to Lake Huron rival those of an ocean and often change radically over the 2 to 3 days most boats need to complete the course. In July the only thing predictable about the weather is that it will likely be unpredictable—at least to some extent. Thunderstorms and squalls, often violent, can rapidly sweep the area, sometimes seemingly faster than radar and the

WingNuts *under sail in 2010. (AP Photo/G. Randall Goss)*

best forecasting can see them coming. Boats are often damaged and crew injured. But for all this, there had never been a race-related death.

Suzanne, Mark, his three co-owners, and three others comprised the crew of *WingNuts*, a modified Kiwi 35, a sailboat that looked very unusual at first view. Like the fast racing boats used in the Volvo Ocean Race and many others, the Kiwi had a lightweight planing hull that was ballasted primarily by a heavy bulb at the bottom of a long, thin keel. At 35 feet, *WingNuts* displaced only some 4,000 pounds, about 1,400 of which was ballast. The primary beam of the hull was only a little over 8 feet, providing minimum wetted surface, and the boat carried a proportionally large amount of sail.

But what made a Kiwi unusual was its "wings," which extended out 3 feet from the hull on both sides, a couple feet above the water. While on a typical race boat the crew sat on the rail on the windward side using their body weight to help keep the boat upright, on a Kiwi the crew could move their whole bodies out of the cockpit far to the side to provide greater leverage. When well balanced by the combined righting forces of the keel and crew weight, the boat could carry more sail without being blown over, and thus sailed very fast.

With a crew of eight on *WingNuts*, it was important to maintain an exact balance of weight. But Mark and his crew were very experienced and had sailed her often enough over 4 years to make their movements a choreographed art. They had also added some 300 pounds to the keel ballast to increase stability.

Sailing on *WingNuts* was very fast—and very exciting.

And they suspected this Chicago–Mac would be an exciting one. A south wind was forecast for the Saturday start, allowing them to fly up the northeast course under a spinnaker. Thunderstorms were predicted for later on Sunday, possibly severe, but they were ready for that too.

Winds remained fairly light most of Saturday, but they enjoyed a good pace with the spinnaker. The eight of them alternated watches, got some sleep, and worked flawlessly as a team. Mark was grinning all the time, and Suzanne smiled whenever she watched him at the helm. She was the only woman on the boat, one of only two crew outside their extended family, but she pulled her weight like everyone else and had earned their respect. One of the great joys of a race like this was the bond everyone felt as they worked together.

Except for the reddish sky at dawn, Sunday began much like Saturday. The wind was still southerly but getting stronger, and *WingNuts* was simply flying under the big spinnaker. Everyone had slept at least some, and the adrenaline countered whatever fatigue might have been setting in. They all felt fine, the younger crew still excited if a little apprehensive about the radio's thunderstorm predictions. Late in the afternoon they saw clouds building to the west.

The storm moved in after sunset, and the wind began clocking around toward the west and building. Lightning flickered to the west and southwest. Gradually the wind increased even more as they watched the radar and saw storm cells moving in. When they put the second reef in the mainsail and changed to the smallest jib, the lightning was so bright they scarcely needed the spreader lights to see what they were doing.

The shifting wind confused the seas and made steering trickier, but they'd trained for this and maintained good control. Except when they were below in the cabin they kept tethered to the jackline down the center of the cockpit. With 6-foot tethers from their harnesses to the jackline, there was no way anyone could go over the side.

Then the wind rose rapidly to 30 knots and beyond and they dropped the main entirely and tied it securely to the boom. The small jib was enough to maintain steerage on port tack. Thunder cracked almost constantly now as *WingNuts* shuddered through the gusts. Windblown rain and spray blasted them from every angle. All they could do was try to keep the boat under control until the storm passed.

Seated on the starboard side, Suzanne was watching forward when off the port bow the blackness between lightning flashes turned white, as if the air had become sudden dense fog. She fingered the titanium knife she always wore on a lanyard around her neck; you never knew when you might have to cut yourself free from a line or even your tether. Above the shrieking wind she heard shouts and saw Mark look up from the bright blob in the center of the radar screen, already scrambling for the jib furling line and jerking it back to roll in the little jib fast, when a terrible gust caught them from port as *WingNuts* came off a wave. The port wing rose up fast and Mark tumbled across the cockpit onto Suzanne as the wing lifted higher, and then they were going over. She grabbed Mark and struggled for a handhold on anything, but the wing was above them now and they went backward in free-fall as everything was blotted out above. The last thing she felt before blacking out was the jerk of her harness on her shoulders and back as the tether snapped tight.

The mast struck the water and kept going. The righting force of the heavy keel bulb raised high above the water was no match for the near-hurricane-force sustained gusts and crashing waves against the port wing. The boat just kept rolling. In a flash it had turtled, and lay upside down in the troubled water.

The lightning helped those struggling under the surface to orient themselves. Quick-release tether snaphooks allowed some to free themselves quickly from their harnesses and surface beside the boat, while others needed help. Everything happened very quickly in the chaos of water and thunder, and the crew was going mostly on instinct, fighting to escape the water. One crew had been in the cabin and had to find his way out and down through the tangle of lines and rigging.

Within a couple of minutes six crew had their heads above water and some were able to clamber up onto the hull. The boat tossed in the waves, and the rain blown hard by the wind was blinding. Peter saw that Mark and Suzanne were still missing and pulled his way around the boat, plunging his head below the surface to look below the boat. At one point he spotted Suzanne under the hull, and in a burst of lightning saw her mouth was open, her eyes open and lifeless. He could not reach her tether to release it but knew it was too late anyway. But there was still hope for Mark, who might be alive in an air pocket beneath the boat or might be drifting in the water nearby.

The other non-family crew clung to the hull thinking of his mother. While pregnant with him she had lost her husband, the father he'd never met, to drowning in another Lake Michigan boating accident.

Crew on the inverted hull had already activated their PLBs (personal locator beacons) when Peter finally gave up his search for Mark. The thunderstorm cell that had struck them was slowly

WingNuts *floating upside down the day after the incident. (AP Photo/John L. Russell)*

moving on, the lightning a little farther away, but the wind was still strong and waves were still washing over the hull. It wasn't dark enough for them to see the running lights of the nearest sailboats, but even though they felt alone in the storm they were blowing the whistles attached to their PFDs and waving their strobes and flashlights.

The crew of a sailboat a half mile away heard their whistles and, although battling the thunderstorm as well, was able to rescue the six *WingNuts* crew long before the Coast Guard's rescue boat and helicopter reached the area. Several other sailboats also joined in the search for anyone missing in the water near the capsized boat.

As soon as the crew of the rescuing boat learned of the missing two sailors, they radioed a request for rescue divers, but Peter knew it was too late. Divers later recovered the bodies of Mark and Suzanne, who was still tethered to the center jackline. Both had suffered head injuries when the boat flipped to starboard and the port-side wing crashed down on them.

••• — — — •••

U.S. Sailing conducted a thorough inquiry and issued a report 3 months later, which some of this retelling is based on. Recommendations from the panel's experts included considerations for increased safety training and safety gear, such as types of tethers, but the most significant issue focused on a sailboat's stability index, or its ability to recover from a knockdown or capsize.

The implications were that WingNuts' crew were well prepared and did everything right but that the boat itself was not an appropriate design for such conditions. In races, the organizers can decide what entries to allow based on the boat, required equipment, crew characteristics and experience, and other factors. In recreational sailing, however, the sailors themselves decide what conditions their own boats, and their own experience and gear, can withstand. These are personal decisions, of course, and sometimes "fluke" accidents do occur, but usually, as most of the stories in this book show, the final outcomes could have been prevented.

Rally Boat to Bermuda

Every fall a large number of cruising boats leave the U.S. East Coast and head for the Caribbean to spend the winter there. Some experienced sailors choose to go on their own, with or without the assistance of professional private weather forecasters and route advisers, while others, often those making this passage for the first time, opt to join one of the organized rallies. The North American Rally to the Caribbean (NARC), which departs Newport, Rhode Island, and generally routes first to Bermuda, is a popular choice for sailors in the Northeast. Rob and Jan Anderson, aboard their Island Packet 380, *Triple Stars*, joined the fall 2011 NARC in part for the comfort and fun of being part of the fleet and in part for the promised weather and route planning expertise.

The Andersons were not inexperienced sailors, however. Years before, they had sailed south from California, through the Panama Canal, and up to Maine, where they had been living before starting their adventure to the Caribbean.

Weather is the major issue for sailors headed south to the islands. First you have to wait for the end of hurricane season, which is why the NARC and the Caribbean 1500, another rally of cruising boats, which leaves from Hampton, Virginia, both begin in November. Then you have to wait for a good weather window between the frequent fall fronts that sweep the northwestern Atlantic. Because the winds are generally from the east when you approach the Caribbean, you need to make your easting before getting too far south, one reason many boats head east first for Bermuda, and then sail almost due south. This route involves planning a course for crossing the Gulf Stream, a violent area in a northerly blow, as well as for avoiding adverse winds and gales on the way to Bermuda.

The 2011 NARC left Newport on November 1 with a promising but narrow weather window and a less than perfect long-range forecast, though conditions are seldom ideal. But it looked reasonable for the 630–nautical mile passage to Bermuda as long as all the rally boats got there before the weather worsened. The Andersons anticipated some high winds and seas but felt confident in their boat and skills. Later there would be some debate about how good the forecasting and route advice actually were.

Triple Stars made good time at first, although slower than most of the boats in the rally, and crossed the Gulf Stream easily. By the fifth day, however, the wind had risen and the Andersons decided to heave-to in order to take no chances and get some needed rest. After all, it was just the two of them, without other crew to stand watch and give them more sleep. Heaving-to is a time-honored method that essentially stops the boat safely, requiring less attention. For 2 days *Triple Stars* drifted slowly while the rest of the rally fleet sailed on. Jan Anderson wrote in her online blog to family and friends, "So far I must say the weather has been stinky . . . the past couple of days have been tough, but we are hove to and resting today . . . we are both good . . . do not worry . . . we are doing fine."

But to the south, a tropical storm was brewing.

On the seventh day they set sail again, heading for Bermuda, which was still hundreds of miles away. For 3 days they had high winds and big seas but were coping.

On November 11, their tenth day of a voyage that typically takes only 6 or 7, the sun broke through clearing skies. The tropical storm had passed, leaving huge waves, and the wind was dropping. Their spirits rose. They were still more than 200 miles from Bermuda, but it looked like they'd passed through the worst of it.

It was so much calmer, in fact, that Jan took the helm without putting on her PFD and tether. She had every confidence in their seaworthy, full-keel boat continuing to ride through the waves.

A little past noon, Rob was coming up the companionway from the cabin where he'd been catching up on some boat work. As he reached the last step Jan suddenly shouted "Look out!" and before he could turn to look, a huge wave slammed the boat and knocked it over.

Rob was thrown violently into the bimini frame, which crumpled under the impact but kept him from going overboard, but Jan was thrown into the water.

As the boat bobbed back upright, he rushed to the helm and spotted her in the water. He immediately deployed the Lifesling, a flotation rescue collar on a long line, and circled back in the boat to pull its line in to Jan. He saw her grab the line about half-way between the flotation collar and the boat. He tightened the circle to get closer, following the standard procedure, but then she went under.

The line went slack. He never saw her again.

He quickly set off their EPIRB and then hit the emergency button on their VHF-DSC radio. He could only pray for help and keep scanning the water for Jan.

A tanker some 20 miles away responded on the radio and immediately diverted toward Rob's location to assist in the search. The Coast Guard began an aerial search. The tanker arrived an hour later and Rob boarded it, abandoning *Triple Stars*, and they continued to search.

After 24 hours the Coast Guard called off its search. Without a PFD or other flotation, Jan could not have survived that long.

••• — — — •••

Why was this experienced sailor not wearing a PFD with a harness and not tethered to the boat? Rob later described the huge wave that hit Triple Stars *as a rogue wave, a sudden, unexpected wave much larger than other passing waves. You don't expect such waves, so you may not be prepared for one to strike without warning.*

As the stories in the following chapters show, however, most sailing emergencies resulting in fatalities do not occur when expected. The greatest danger, you could say, is not expecting danger.

Briefly

Tynemouth, UK, 1998. The skipper of a 14-meter sailboat was taking nine paying guests out for a day sail, even though a gale warning was in effect. He gave a safety briefing but left it to his passengers to decide whether to wear life jackets. Conditions were rough, and within a couple of hours they turned back. As they entered the river harbor, the heavy seas from the earlier gale against the ebbing tide produced large breaking waves, and the boat pitchpoled. Three people, none of them wearing a life jacket, were washed overboard. One was found alive by rescuers; two drowned. The skipper was arrested on a manslaughter charge.

San Francisco, California, May 2010. A couple in their fifties on a weekend cruise in their 33-foot sailboat was approaching the Golden Gate Bridge during only mildly stormy conditions— 25 knots of wind and 8-foot seas. Wrestling their boat through the choppy seas, both fell or were washed overboard. A waiter at the Cliff House restaurant saw the boat in distress and called the Coast Guard, which had a search boat on the scene in less than an hour. One body was found in the water, and the other washed ashore the next day.

Atlantic Ocean, November 2010. A 73-year-old solo sailor encountered a storm some 50 miles offshore east of Florida. His boat's mast broke in a knockdown and he lost engine power. The sailor did not have an EPIRB but got off a VHF Mayday call before his batteries went dead, which luckily was heard by a ship at sea. The search had to cover a huge area of ocean, but with more good luck the boat was located—with the sailor still alive—after a few days.

Pacific Ocean, December 2010. Two men from British Columbia, Canada, were sailing in the Pacific off Costa Rica when their 42-foot trimaran was hit by a storm and started to break up in the battering waves. They had only minutes to abandon ship into an inflatable dinghy before the boat sank. Fortunately they had an EPIRB, although there was some confusion in the international search-and-rescue effort, resulting in their drifting for 3 days without food or water before being rescued.

Atlantic Ocean, September 2011. Four French sailors in a 36-foot sailboat capsized in a storm some 1,400 miles northeast of Provincetown, Massachusetts. The boat was dismasted, but they had an EPIRB aboard. The Canadian rescue center in Halifax and Coast Guard Boston responded, and a Canadian airplane dropped a sea rescue kit that included a life raft. Thanks to the automated mutual-assistance vessel rescue system (AMVER), an oil rig tender nearest their position soon reached and rescued the sailors. The Coast Guard commended the sailors for having appropriate safety gear aboard.

Atlantic Ocean, November 2011. A 41-foot sailboat left Martha's Vineyard, Massachusetts, for Bermuda with a crew of three. While in the Gulf Stream they encountered unexpected severe weather and waves to 30 feet. The boat was rolled and dismasted while two crew were below; the third ended up in the water, injured and tangled in the rigging. The other two were unable to get him back on board, and he was lost to the sea. Without an EPIRB or a working engine, the other two drifted in the Atlantic for 12 days until, by chance, a tanker passed close enough to see their handheld flares.

CHAPTER 2

Some Incidents Can't Be Prevented?

A fter any sailing fatality, questions are asked that center on one primary issue: could it have been prevented? In the huge majority of cases, sadly, the usual answer is yes. The sailor might have acted more wisely, used appropriate equipment, taken evasive action, or avoided the situation entirely. In many cases, the answer is as simple as wearing a PFD; as many stories in this book show, even if the incident itself could not have been prevented, the victim would likely have survived if he or she had remained afloat. Other situations are more complex and raise deeper questions, such as the three stories in this chapter. All involve what is often called a fluke accident, pure chance, like being struck by lightning. The only way to be 100% certain of avoiding lightning is to never be where it strikes—never to sail at all. For a sailor, that's about as likely as never getting in a car or never going outdoors. And just as chance sometimes seems to play a role in whether an incident occurs, chance also seems to affect whether the individual lives or dies. Yet "chance" seems too simple an explanation, even in the rarer instances where it may be true, and it is always worthwhile to ask the hard questions, to consider all the factors involved, to develop better gear or training or rules. Ultimately opinions will differ, but the acts of asking and considering the options make us all better, and safer, sailors.

Tangled in Rigging

The 420 is a centerboard dinghy designed to be sailed by two. At 4.2 meters length overall, with a beam of 1.6 meters, it carries a substantial sail area for its light displacement (80 kilograms) and easily reaches planing speed. It's a popular boat for youth training and racing and has been a world-class racer since 1975, a youth stepping stone to the Olympic 470.

The Club 420 is a slightly heavier version that is more commonly sailed in North America, typically in sailing schools, yacht clubs, and collegiate sailing programs. Usually sailed by youth using a mainsail and jib, the Club 420 may also be raced using a spinnaker and one-person trapeze. The trapeze consists of a line or wire from the masthead to a harness worn by the more forward crew to balance the boat against heeling when sailing upwind, as shown in the photo. When the trapeze is not in use, the trapeze

These 420 sailors are racing using a trapeze. (U.S. Junior Women's Double-Handed Sailing in 2008. Photo courtesy of the Sausalito Yacht Club race committee boat cameraperson, Roxanne Fairbairn.)

wire and its hook are secured near the mast. Significant skill and athleticism are required to use the trapeze.

At age 14, Olivia was a happy young woman, a varsity soccer player at her Maryland high school, and said by friends to be easy-going and carefree. She loved music and sports. Already a skilled sailor, she was a member of her school's sailing team and was very experienced in the Optimist dinghy. As part of her training she'd learned and practiced how to right both an Opti and a 420 following a capsize.

In June 2011, she was sailing the 420 as crew for Sarah, another young member of their racing club. This was the first week of practice for them on the Club 420 in their summer sailing camp, and they were training with Arthur, their certified sailing instructor and coach.

On this day they were to practice with the spinnaker down-wind and the trapeze upwind. While Olivia had not yet practiced with the trapeze, she had already sailed the 420 in winds stronger than today. With Sarah on the tiller, Olivia would manage both the spinnaker and the trapeze. The wind on the Chesapeake was good for practice, 5 to 10 knots south to west with only light puffs. Olivia put on her life jacket and adjusted the trapeze harness, for later use, around her waist. She got in the boat and raised the sail.

Once sailing, they found wind shifts a little stronger than they'd anticipated, but nothing more than they'd encountered before. Their coach set them and the other boats on a windward-leeward race course for the practice.

After rounding the windward mark, Olivia set the spinnaker on starboard tack. As the wind behind them shifted, they oscillated between a run and a broad reach, Sarah steering to prevent a jibe while Olivia trimmed the spinnaker.

Well before the leeward mark they prepared to douse the spinnaker. Sitting on the port side, Sarah turned a little farther off the wind to blanket the spinnaker behind the mainsail to lower the pressure on it. Forward on the starboard side, Olivia slid up beside the mast and reached forward and started pulling down the spinnaker.

The sail was almost halfway down when on a sudden wind shift the boat accidentally jibed. The boom swung fast across the cockpit and the boat heeled sharply to starboard. Olivia was pushed farther forward and out to the side by the boom as the boat heeled but did not tumble backward into the water. Something seemed to hold her on the boat.

As the port rail rose higher, Sarah leaned back as far as she could, trying to use her weight to counteract the heeling and prevent a capsize. But the boat was rolling too fast and she went into the water as she reached for the centerboard.

In her life jacket Sarah bobbed right back up. She moved along the hull to grab the centerboard as the boat continued rolling, but the hull was turning turtle already. She reached up, got a grip on the centerboard, worked her toes up onto the rail, and stood. But her weight was not enough to make any difference by herself, and the hull remained inverted.

But where was Olivia?

It had been only a few seconds since the capsize and she should have surfaced by now. Sarah looked all around, saw Arthur watching from the fast boat not far off, and waved frantically at him. Immediately he started over. She pulled herself higher on the hull, trying to see into the murky water on the other side of the hull for Olivia, for a hand, anything. Should she dive under? She reached for her life jacket buckles, then looked again into the water, a thick brown-green, and realized there was little she could do alone, plus their coach was almost there. Olivia may have already floated up into the air pocket beneath the capsized hull.

When Arthur arrived and could keep watch, Sarah pulled herself down under the water, still wearing her life jacket, and into the inverted cockpit. On the other side she found Olivia, not moving, and tried to maneuver her up to the air pocket, but she was stuck on something. After several futile efforts she swam back out to get their coach.

Arthur had already radioed for help and now jumped in to attempt to free Olivia. She was tangled in the rigging, but the water was too murky to see exactly how she was held. Her trapeze harness had hung up on the hook and twisted around so that he couldn't at first release it under the pressure.

Finally he freed it, and they pulled her out and got her quickly into another boat that had responded. He guessed it had been only 4 or 5 minutes since the capsize, but she had no pulse. They started CPR immediately as the boat raced for shore. The 911 call had already been made. An ambulance arrived shortly after they reached shore, and the paramedics took over. Everything possible was done in the ambulance and hospital emergency department, but resuscitation efforts failed.

••• — — — •••

While any accidental death is tragic, Olivia's seems particularly so. She was young and had done nothing wrong. It seemed as randomly cruel and pointless as a lightning strike—worse, even, as she would have sought safe harbor if lightning had threatened.

Her story was prominent in the news and sailing media for a long time. Inevitably, discussion focused on a range of issues, including equipment, training, age, the responsibilities of sailing schools, safety procedures, and even the nature of risk in any sport. Some speculated that inexperience may have contributed to the accidental jibe or the problem with the trapeze equipment, or possibly that fear caused Olivia to freeze when the problem arose. U.S. Sailing, the governing body for organized racing in the United States, conducted an independent review and issued a lengthy, thoughtful report. It found no fault by anyone involved, and while it made a series of general recommendations for the sport of sailing, it remains far from clear whether this tragedy could have been avoided if anything had been done differently.

Lost Keel

The Fastnet! What sailor of age doesn't know of the Fastnet Race? What sailor who races, who reads, or who simply was in tune with the world in 1979 doesn't remember the world's worst sailing disaster and the largest peacetime water-rescue operation? That year, with over 300 boats participating, a severe storm with unexpected hurricane-force winds swept in and decimated the fleet. Fewer than 90 boats finished the race. Almost 200 quit the race to seek shelter. Two dozen boats were caught in the worst of it and were sunk, crippled, or abandoned. Well over 100 sailors were rescued in an effort spearheaded by the Royal Navy and involving literally thousands of personnel. Fifteen sailors died.

The race runs over 600 nautical miles on the offshore waters off England and Ireland. It has generally been held every 2 years since 1925 and is the culminating event for many professional racers. Several books have been written about it and the 1979 race. In 1985 another dramatic rescue was needed when the keel of a maxi yacht broke off and the boat turtled, trapping six crew for a time under the inverted hull.

The reputation of the Fastnet, then, is inevitably on the minds of all sailors entering the race. It's something you can't help but think about, no matter your experience and background. Regardless of your level of professionalism, you prepare for the Fastnet, and you make sure your boat and equipment—and crew—are all ready for what may come.

So it was that in 2011 the skipper of *Rambler 100* and his 20 crew prepared well for the August race. All were highly experienced, several had sailed in America's Cup races, and just weeks before they had sailed *Rambler* across the Atlantic, winning another race in record time. Compared to the conditions they had experienced then, given the forecast for this Fastnet, some of them might even have viewed this race as a piece of cake. They had a great boat, a great crew, and every expectation of another win.

At 100 feet overall, the super-maxi *Rambler*, one of the world's fastest monohull sailboats, had a high-tech contemporary design, including movable water ballast and a canting keel to balance a huge sail plan. *Canting* means that the long, thin keel with a weighted bulb on the bottom does not simply hang straight down off the bottom of the hull but can be angled up on the windward side to prevent the boat being blown over. Almost half the boat's total weight of over 70,000 pounds was condensed into the bulb at the bottom of the keel, hanging some 18 feet underwater.

Nothing unusual happened in the first part of the race. In fact, winds in the low 20s made it almost relaxing compared to conditions they'd experienced before. At five o'clock in the afternoon when they rounded Fastnet Rock, four crew were off watch below. Several others relaxed on deck while the on-watch crew did their job to maximize boat speed. Waves were 5 to 6 feet, and *Rambler* launched off the bigger ones and pounded along after a turn upwind.

Then the crew below heard a terrible crack and grind as the keel broke off when *Rambler* came off a wave. With all the sound and fury on deck, most of the crew there didn't realize what had happened until *Rambler* started going over.

There was a brief pause when the mast and sails hit the water, then the rolling continued. In less than a minute *Rambler* had turned turtle, floating upside down, the broken keel stub pointing skyward as the hull pitched in the waves.

A few of the crew managed to climb over the rail and onto the bottom of the hull as it rolled. All the rest were in the water, including the four who had been below and who had been unable to grab life jackets in the chaos of the cabin rotating 180 degrees before struggling out of the cabin and swimming free of the tangle of underwater rigging and lines.

Luckily no one was caught in the rigging or otherwise pinned under the boat.

The auto-inflate function of the crews' inflatable PFDs had been disabled to prevent buoyancy from trapping them under the boat. This function is designed to protect a sailor who is knocked unconscious and is thus unable to pull the cord manually for inflation. Fortunately all 21 sailors were conscious and those wearing them were able to inflate their PFDs. Later, when giving their recommendations based on this experience, the crew urged not using auto-inflate PFDs. While this does not seem a controversial

Rambler's crew on its inverted hull awaiting rescue. (Photo copyright RNLI)

issue in this instance, there have been other emergencies in which unconscious sailors were saved by their auto-inflating PFDs.

Similarly, perhaps in part because they were not in storm conditions and thus not at particular risk of being washed or thrown overboard, none of the crew was clipped on to the boat with a tether. In this case, again, this reduced the risk of being caught under the boat and unable to get free quickly. But again, many other sailors in other emergencies have been saved by their use of a harness and tether to keep them on the boat.

Immediately after the capsize, the crew began climbing up out of the water onto the inverted hull, assisted by those who had managed to stay on the boat. As professional sailors, many of whom in the past had raced dinghies and were experienced with capsizes, they maintained a sense of calm that might have surprised most recreational sailors in such circumstances.

Within minutes, 16 crew were out of the cold water on the relative safety of the hull. Five, including the skipper, were missing. The others quickly conferred and were fairly certain none of the missing was trapped below; someone remembered seeing each of the missing crew free in the water. Hopefully they were all okay and had just drifted away from the boat and would be found by the rescuers they assumed would arrive soon since the crew on the hull had already activated the signals of the two PLBs they had with them.

Here again, some would say they were fortunate. Each of the 21 crew had a PLB, but because conditions had not been viewed as risky, only two crew had their PLBs on them.

Since they had capsized on the race course, they hoped another boat would pass close enough to see them. If only they'd been able to grab a handheld VHF radio! One crew had been able to make a quick Mayday call on a handheld VHF as the boat rolled, but he'd lost it when swimming clear after the capsize. He'd had no chance to relay their position, and the radio was not DSC equipped, which would have automatically provided their GPS coordinates to other boats in the area.

The boat's satellite phone, as well, was somewhere down below. As was the EPIRB. And the life rafts were unreachable if needed.

Although visibility was poor, they soon saw another sailboat passing. The crew on the inverted hull shouted, waved their arms and strobe lights, and blew the whistles attached to their PFDs but the boat raced past.

Another was sighted and it too passed. In the first hour they watched helplessly as four boats sailed past without hearing or seeing them perched on the hull floating low in the water.

After 2 hours, some of the crew must have been wondering if the PLBs were working. Their signals should have been received and rescue boats should have arrived by now. Although they were wet and cold in the wind, their thoughts were for the five crew still out there in the water. The water temperature was in the high 50s (°F), cold enough for hypothermia to set in.

Then a lifeboat arrived. The crew on the hull sent it off to look for those missing in the water, but it soon returned, saying other rescue boats were searching for them now and a radio call had gone out to all boats to assist. The 16 were ferried over to the lifeboat.

Forty-five minutes later, the five crew were found a short distance away. They had linked arms and huddled together to preserve body heat. Only one experienced hypothermia severe enough to require being airlifted to a hospital, and she was released later in good condition.

Everyone was safe. Except for a short delay resulting from some confusion about the PLB signals, the rescue effort had gone very well.

••• — — — •••

Even in a story that ends well, however, there is speculation about what might have happened and what can be done to help ensure the next story ends as well; that is, to leave nothing to chance or luck. Recommendations in the U.S. Sailing Safety at Sea Review emphasized that crew should always have a PLB- or DSC-equipped handheld VHF on their person as well as a bright strobe light or laser flare, and they should ensure that other boat safety equipment is always accessible in any emergency.

Or in a phrase, even in calm conditions, think about "what if" scenarios and be prepared.

Keep Treading!

"For God's sake, girl!"

Her voice sounded weird in the dark, almost like someone else speaking. She almost spun around in the pitch black to see who else was there. She was losing it. "What, already?" She shouted this time, and now heard how her chattering teeth distorted her voice.

"Goddamn, it's cold!"

There, that was better. She almost grinned in the dark, but a wave splashed in her mouth and she had to spit it out. She stopped treading for a moment then and felt her body slip lower in the water. She was so cold.

She barely felt her muscles now, but knew they were still moving because she wasn't sinking. Yet. "Go, girl!"

Part of her couldn't believe she was talking to herself, shouting actually, like some sort of crazed cheerleader.

And she still couldn't believe what had happened and that now she was all alone in the cold, dark water some 50 nautical miles off Cornwall, England. The boat was long gone. It had been hours—at least that's what it felt like.

She didn't even have a life jacket to keep her floating until the cold killed her. "Damn you!" she shouted again. Shouting helped hold off the terror, if only for a few seconds.

"Paddle, girl!" A wave splashed over her head. "You will *not* kill me like this!"

If only there were stars. Stars would give enough light to at least show the waves around her. But the sky was as dark as ink.

Shouldn't there have been a helicopter by now? "Where are you?" Surely it couldn't take so long.

If only she'd worn a watch. Then she could keep track, do calculations, keep up hope while she waited. Surely they'd radioed. "The damn GPS was working, wasn't it?" She rolled back and changed her stroke, felt her body again. Still working.

When she was quiet too long, the terror returned. It came over her in waves, over and over, always beginning with the horror of abruptly realizing she had been trapped under the boat. In the black water she had been completely disoriented, unable to see or tell up from down, just aware she was underwater and caught on something. She had struggled and torn at the harness webbing of her inflated PFD and tether, and suddenly her fingers found the release and freed her from her PFD. The rushing water had torn her free, and moments later she had bobbed up behind the boat to see its stern light rapidly receding into the night.

It had been all she could do after the sudden immersion to stay on the surface and suck air into her lungs between coughing fits. She heard men on the boat shouting in the distance but was unable to shout back.

She watched the boat disappear, then a minute later saw its green starboard light moving left to right, but it was too far away to hear her shouting. If only she had a light, but her strobe, like her whistle, was clipped to her PFD.

As far as she knew, her PFD was still under the boat. Or maybe by now they'd pulled it up by her tether, still connected to the starboard jackline, which must have been loose to let her go that far under, and found it empty. Maybe they thought she was dead by now.

"I will *not* die this way!" she shouted into the void around her.

She saw the boat make another sweep, right to left this time, with the port red running light showing, but it was still a long way off. She saw it only for a second, from the crest of a wave, and then she dropped down in the trough and the boat was gone when she rose again. The seas were running perhaps 3 to 4 meters; they'd practically have to run her over to see her.

She would die if the helicopter didn't find her soon. Very soon, she thought, then screamed, "No!"

And the terror of being caught under the boat swept over her yet again.

She tried to keep it out of her mind, tried to remember more about what had happened. How far out had they been? How far could a helicopter fly before going back for more fuel?

She'd been in the cockpit one minute, enjoying the wild ride, loving the roar of water along the hull, grinding the winch to trim in the jib, and then something happened and she'd slid under the lifeline. Just like that. She couldn't remember how it had happened. Just the abrupt horror of being held underwater, against her will, as if the sea had become a madman.

Don't think about that part of it. "Girl! Keep paddling!" And she'd lost her PFD. She thought about that: the strobe light, the whistle, the big inflated tube to float her high and keep the water out of her mouth, a lovely bright yellow tube that would glow like the sun in the helicopter's searchlight.

Don't think about how the helicopter might not see her when it arrived. "Stop it! It's going to find me!"

She was beyond cold. She wasn't sure what her arms and legs were doing now, she was only aware of their leaden weight. She'd kicked off her sailing boots and later her jacket, which had made it so difficult to tread water. But now she felt just as heavy in the water. How much easier it would be just to lean back and let it all slip away.

Her mouth filled with water and she jerked up, thrashing her arms, coughing, then shouted at the sea, "Damn you!"

How long had it been now? What had happened to time?

She had a crazy thought: if a person shouts in the middle of the ocean and there's no one there to hear them, do they actually make a sound?

Then she panicked a moment when she suddenly felt she'd gone blind. It was so dark she couldn't tell if her eyes were open. But when she rose on a big wave and kicked hard to look around, she found what looked like sky glow on a horizon. Was the cloud cover lifting? Or was it the glow of distant city lights?

But it was gone on the next wave crest, and she screamed in frustration.

You couldn't live for hours in cold like this. She wondered how she'd even know when she died.

"Girl! Stop it!"

She started counting waves to stay focused. As she rose on each crest she shouted its number and looked for the horizon. She could make it to 100, she knew. She would!

Sometime after 300 she lost track. She felt confused. But she shouted out a number on each wave nonetheless.

"Seventy!" On the horizon was a tiny red light.

"Eighty-three!" Was she hallucinating? The red light was back, and just to the left of it was a tiny green dot.

"Thirty-one! Hey!" She wasn't crazy after all; there was a red and a green light together. Running lights! A boat, coming at her!

"Eighteen!" She barely got it out, not sure why she was crying, her voice breaking, the tears running down her wet salty face feeling warm. "God! A boat!"

She could barely believe it, she *would* believe it—rising on each crest to see it coming straight on—a light on the masthead now clear, a sailboat! Another sailboat coming home from the races?

She stopped shouting now, thinking to save her energy until it came closer, but she couldn't help congratulating herself. "You go, girl!"

She watched while it came closer.

At the crest of a big wave she started shouting for all she was worth and heard a man's voice shout back.

A minute later they were playing a spotlight over the water and she managed to raise one arm to wave and still tread water with the other. The light found her.

She discovered she was still counting waves with meaningless numbers.

They had her aboard for only a few minutes, just long enough to wrap her in blankets, before the first lifeboat arrived, followed soon by a helicopter. One man in the lifeboat had a worried face, and was saying something about it not being good that she wasn't shivering, and then they had her in a sling and were lifting her up to the helicopter.

The roar of the blades was like the roar of water beneath the hull and the terror struck again—until the basket was swung inside and the door slammed shut and a warm hand took hers.

She drifted off, murmuring—they told her later—what sounded like a string of numbers.

When she was released from the hospital a day later, uninjured, she was able to smile at her friends. When they asked what it was like and how she'd survived more than 2 hours of extreme cold, she could only say that she'd just told herself to.

The Tether Issue—An Opinion

I chose the preceding three stories for this chapter because they all involve what many consider a fluke or chance. The sailors who lived or died in these incidents did nothing overtly wrong, regardless of any debate about whether the incident could or could not have been prevented.

However, these stories do raise issues about using harnesses and tethers and the risk of becoming trapped. Some have suggested that being tethered to a boat adds an unnecessary risk, particularly if the boat turns turtle or if there are a sufficient number of crew aboard to rescue a sailor who goes overboard. Yet an overwhelming number of other incidents, including many in the following chapters, show a greater risk of becoming separated from the boat due to a wide range of circumstances.

The 21 sailors aboard *Rambler* who all survived the boat's sudden capsize all subsequently recommended against using a tether. Consider, however, that the risk of being thrown or washed overboard is, for keelboat sailors, far greater than the risk of having your boat's keel break off. Even when capsized the boat will generally bob back upright, bringing to the surface a properly tethered sailor.

Consider also the assumption that a crew overboard will be rescued by sailors still on board. (Obviously this doesn't apply to singlehanders, as we'll see in Chapter 10.) Most offshore sailors do wear a PFD—at least sometimes—and have attached to it a strobe light or whistle to make it easier to be found. PLBs are also being used more frequently. Chartplotters almost universally have a crew-overboard button to instantly record the location where someone goes overboard. And most offshore racing and rally rules require carrying a tall crew-overboard pole to be thrown overboard to help mark the location.

All of this may give the impression that if someone goes over it's simply a matter of turning the boat to pick them up.

How safe is it to assume that?

While this book was being written in 2012, one of the worst American sailing disasters in recent decades occurred during the Farallones Race off San Francisco. An unexpectedly large wave struck a 38-foot boat, sweeping six of the eight crew overboard. Winds were about 25 knots, not unusual for the area, and certainly not storm conditions. All were wearing PFDs. The two still on board immediately focused on getting the others back on the boat when another large wave struck, sending one of them overboard and knocking the boat out of control. Waves soon swept it onto nearby rocks. Immediately an emergency call was made and a Coast Guard rescue effort began. A helicopter rescued three crew and recovered one body.

An extensive search continued the rest of the afternoon, through the night, and all the next day for the four who were still missing. When there was no longer the slightest hope that they could have survived that long in the frigid water, the Coast Guard discontinued the search after it became obvious no more survivors would be found.

Several weeks later one of the three survivors wrote a personal account of the disaster to correct inaccuracies in news reports, and he concluded with thoughtful reflections about the importance of using a tether. Like the others, he had not been clipped in and his time in the water had been terrifying. But tethering shouldn't be a personal choice, he argued, because even one person overboard puts the whole crew at risk when they have to act to attempt a rescue.

Three months after the incident, the investigation team of U.S. Sailing published its report. Two of the safety issues cited were a "failure of seamanship in negotiating shoal waters on a lee shore" and "inadequate safety gear for offshore conditions," including the use of appropriate PFDs and tethers. It quoted the U.S. Sailing Prescription recommendation in the ISAF Offshore Special Regulations that tethers should "be employed whenever conditions warrant, and always in rough weather, on cold water, or at night, or under conditions of reduced visibility or when sailing short-handed."

CHAPTER 3

A Good Day's Sail Goes Bad

F or most sailors, sailing in a good wind on a day with good weather is one of the great joys in life. You're out in the natural world, feeling the warmth of the sun over the cool of the water, feeling the breeze on your face and the boat's responses to natural forces, enjoying time away from land and all that entails, enjoying a time either social or solitary—and often feeling a great peacefulness. You may also thrill to the adrenaline of a race or simply the challenge of controlling your boat through continually changing circumstances. There may be as many ways to enjoy sailing as there are sailors; we all have our own experiences and joys. But in the back of our minds we must remember that water is not humans' natural environment and that whenever we are on the water we are at some risk. This mindfulness isn't fear and needn't detract from the pleasure in any way, and can actually enhance the joy of sailing, but it is needed if we are to stay safe in case something unexpected happens. And as these stories show, the unexpected happens often.

Remember, too, that regardless of how warm the water or air may seem there is always some risk of hypothermia. People in cold water may have as little as 10 minutes of functional movement before losing the effective use of their fingers, arms, and legs, making drowning a risk even for a good swimmer who believes he or she can tread water until rescue arrives.

Just One Little Mistake

"Great day for sailing, eh?" Dave was grinning as he came down the dock with his brown lab, Rusty.

Shannon looked up from the cockpit, smiled, then gestured out at Chesapeake Bay, where not a boat was in sight. "Nice day for December, anyway," she said.

Rusty, a good boat dog, bounded down into the cockpit and sniffed the bag that held their lunch.

The handheld VHF clipped to Dave's belt was tuned to NOAA weather, and the robotic voice was forecasting a southwest wind of 10 to 15 knots. The report from the nearest automated buoy included an air temperature of 54°F, a water temperature of 47°F, and a chop of 1 to 2 feet.

"Won't break any speed records today," Dave said. "Too bad."

Shannon stowed the last of her gear. "That's better for Steve, anyway. Don't want to scare the bejeebers out of him on his first sail."

Dave laughed. It felt great to sneak away from work for a half-day sail, and there was maybe only one other thing he'd rather be doing with Shannon. He stepped down into the cockpit and gave her a quick kiss. "Maybe we shouldn't wait for him after all," he joked.

Steve arrived a few minutes later, but they barely recognized him at first under all that clothing. Dave had told him it would be cold on the water, but he hadn't anticipated Steve would wear a ski parka, heavy gloves, and a winter stocking cap. He saw them looking at his cap—they, so experienced, in their high-tech miracle fabrics—and said, "Gotta stay warm! But I brought some cold beer in case we get too warm."

Rusty trotted over to sniff Steve's bag and then his boots.

Steve was older than both of them, in his forties, Shannon guessed. A whole generation older, almost. He was also a very big man. She stared at his heavy black-soled boots as he gingerly stepped over the rail and down onto the cockpit bench, imagining black scuff marks all over her new boat's gleaming white deck. Oh, well.

Steve dropped his bag into the small cabin of the 18-foot sloop, and Shannon pointed to where he should sit. She swung the engine mount down to lower the outboard into the water and started it. She caught Steve's eye and pointed at the life jacket on the seat. "Better put that on."

Steve glanced at her, then at Dave. Dave was wearing his usual old, stained life jacket.

Dave untied the bow line and came aboard after releasing the stern line, holding on to a deck cleat to keep the boat from drifting.

Steve wasn't able to get even one arm into the life jacket over his bulky parka. Shannon made a face at Dave, then said to Steve, "You'll have to put it on underneath your coat. Loosen the adjustment straps first."

A minute later they were motoring out of the marina into the fresh sunny air, and her spirits rose. It wasn't far to open water and a clear breeze. There's nothing half as fine, she used to say, as turning off a sailboat's engine. She only half listened as Dave explained to Steve how sailing worked. Actually, she noticed, he wasn't saying much about sailing but more about how Steve should keep out of their way and always sit where he was told. Good! On a boat displacing only 1,100 pounds, of which only 300 were ballast, the position of Steve's weight mattered. From his puzzled eyes she guessed he'd never been on a sailboat and had no idea the boat would heel. She always got a kick out of seeing newbies' faces the first time they thought the boat was tipping over.

Rusty finally settled down on the cockpit sole, resting his big square jaw on her feet. He was never an issue with just Dave and her, but today might be a problem. Maybe Dave could get him to stay in the cabin.

Once in open water, she turned up into the wind and Dave rattled up the mainsail and cleated off the halyard. With the mainsheet in tight, she fell off onto a starboard tack and shut off the outboard. As she eased down the centerboard, the sloop began making way, water gurgling at the stern. Ah, the feel of the tiller in her hand; she thought she could probably sail blindfolded just by the touch!

Dave unfurled the 150% genoa with the sheet in one hand while he let out the furling line with the other. Then he trimmed the sheet in hard and the boat heeled over and picked up speed—and there was the look of panic in Steve's eyes as he grabbed at the lifeline at his back. She grinned.

The wind was forecast to be 10 to 15 knots but it couldn't have been over 8 or 9 yet, and she was happy again that she had splurged for the big genoa. Summer winds in the Chesapeake were often light and she really needed it then, but she always looked forward to the better wind of fall and winter.

For a couple of hours they simply sailed about in big, lazy circles, Dave explaining about tacks and jibes and shifting your weight from one side to the other and keeping your head down below the boom. Steve caught on—he wasn't stupid, she could tell—but he was big and slow moving. Tacking was like a circus fire drill. Steve sat on the windward side forward with Shannon at the tiller beside him, both their feet tangling with Rusty, who wouldn't stay below. Dave took the leeward cockpit bench, leaning against the cabin bulkhead and keeping his feet out of the dog tangle. When they tacked, Steve lumbered across in front of Dave so he could keep his hold on the cabin top while Dave danced around trying to control the sheets from behind him and avoid stepping on Rusty.

Last time we do it this way! she thought. Now she was glad there were no other boats around to see their little zoo in action.

She put them on a long beam reach out and down the bay, and they ate sandwiches and Steve had a beer. Gradually the wind was coming up, maybe 12 to 13 knots now, and she was enjoying their speed on the fast reach. She leaned back and felt the sun on her face while Dave and Steve talked. The combination of chilly air and warm sun was delightful.

But all too soon it was time to head back. They came about and trimmed to a beam reach on port tack. Rusty was getting restless now—he had to pee but wouldn't on the boat—and kept standing up and trying to climb onto the cockpit seats. The boat just wasn't big enough for all of them. Fortunately the wind was up now and they were zipping back; well, she thought, what passes for zipping in an 18-footer with a stubby keel. It had gotten gusty, too, and she was having fun playing the tiller, falling off and heading up to avoid too much heeling. Dave was teaching Steve about sail trim now, explaining what to do with the sheets when you changed course or the wind changed.

Steve had the mainsheet in his hand when the first harder gust hit them. Shannon didn't have time to respond with the tiller, and they heeled hard over for a long moment. Someone's foot kicked Rusty, and he squealed and tried to climb up onto Steve's lap on the windward side. Steve was trying to stand and push Rusty off and eased the mainsheet without noticing what he was doing. The boat flattened and slowed. Steve stood up in the middle of the cockpit and had just brought the sheet back in some when the next gust hit.

"Let out the sheet!" Shannon shouted. Steve looked at the line in his hand as the boat started to heel, and then Rusty was sliding across the cockpit bench, nails screeching on the fiberglass as he banged into Steve. Holding the sheet firmly, Steve lost his balance as the boat heeled and pitched leeward on top of Dave.

Steve's hand had a death grip on the mainsheet, and the weight of his body pulled the sail in all the way.

Feet braced across the cockpit, her weight now the only ballast to windward, Shannon instinctively pulled with all her strength on the tiller to fall off before the boat went over. There was no time for the awareness to sink in that with the main tight, it would've been better just to turn into the wind. But it was already too late. Steve was struggling to hold on as the rail went under, Rusty was flailing against the leeward lifeline, Dave was trying to grab Rusty before the water washed him off, the cockpit was flooding, and the rudder had no bite as it lifted out of the water and they went over.

It happened so fast and the water was so cold that when she broke the surface a moment later she was utterly confused, unsure where she was. Where was the boat? Treading water, she twisted and found it behind her. It had not bounced back upright as it should have but had settled on its side like a seagull with a broken wing.

Abruptly she was shocked into awareness. In his PFD, Dave was beside the hull, holding on to something with one hand, fumbling in the water with his other. Beside him Rusty scratched at the hull with his front paws, trying to climb up the smooth fiberglass.

Then Dave was shouting "Mayday, Mayday, Mayday!" and she saw the handheld radio at his mouth. A moment later, Rusty gave up on the hull and tried to put his paws on Dave's shoulders—as they had played so often in the water—and then Dave wasn't shouting and she couldn't see the radio anymore.

The water was really, really cold and she couldn't think.

Then Dave swam to her side and pulled her back to the boat, but it had settled much lower in the water and seemed to be going down. Sailboats aren't supposed to sink, she thought dully. They always say just stay with the boat until rescue comes. But somehow this one was filling with water and sinking.

Suddenly she realized she hadn't seen Steve. There he was, farther along the hull, his head barely held out of the water by the life jacket. His eyes were open and slowly blinking, his face pale; he was just floating, not speaking. At least he seemed okay.

"Here!" Dave was shouting in her ear. "Take it—put it on!" She turned back to him as he shoved his life jacket to her. "Put it on—I can swim forever."

She realized then that she was barely able to keep treading water, her arms and legs moving slowly. Water splashed in her mouth and she spat it out, then she grabbed the life jacket and hugged it to her chest, grateful just to hang on for a moment.

Dave was calling for Rusty as he swam off. She turned slowly in the water. The boat, her boat, was gone!

Only with difficulty could she see Steve, still bobbing silently in place.

But you're supposed to stay with the boat, she kept thinking, so it's easier for the rescuers to see you. The rescuers. How would they see them now? Then a sickening realization: Dave had not had time to tell them where they were.

Out of the morass of cold and confusion and growing terror came a thought: her cell phone. In her pants pocket. Inside a ziplock bag to protect against spray and splashes.

She had to get the life jacket on first so she could call. The rescuers didn't know where they were. She had to tell them. She had to get the life jacket on.

She fought to get one arm through, her head going underwater. But it hung up on her jacket, she couldn't get her other arm in, she had to breathe, and she jerked it off to clutch it again to her chest as she tried to catch her breath. Her fingers were getting numb, she suddenly realized, and she was seized by a new terror of not being able to push the right buttons on the phone.

She couldn't wait. Clutching the life jacket tight with one arm, she fished in her pocket with the other hand and felt the slick plastic around the phone. Carefully she drew it out and raised it out of the water. Held it against the sky, shaking off the water; it looked dry inside.

Don't fuck it up now, she ordered herself, and took a moment to plan her moves. The waves were only a foot high, only sometimes splashing her face, so if she opened the bag and held it over her head it should stay dry. She could shout at them, she didn't have to put it to her ear to listen.

Moving slowly, she maneuvered the life jacket under her left arm and squeezed it tight in her armpit. She had to lean over to balance her head above the water with both her hands raised, but it worked. She waited a moment, calming herself. She could get her left hand only a few inches over the water, but she carefully opened the ziplock bag, then held the cell higher in her free right hand. With her thumb she keyed 9-1-1, then raised the cell and started shouting. "Mayday, Mayday, Mayday! Our boat has sunk! We're in the water! We're about 2 miles west of Hardy's Marina.

Mayday! Two miles west of Hardy's Marina. We're in the water . . ." she shouted until a wave splashed in her mouth and she coughed.

When she caught her breath again, she looked up at the phone. Its screen was blank. It was wet. She pressed keys and nothing happened.

Had it worked? Had they heard?

She didn't know. She was so cold she couldn't think straight. Then it struck her like a blinding pain in the head: why had she opened the bag at all, why didn't she just talk through the plastic? God!

She lowered her hand slowly and looked at the cell. Wet. She let it slip from her fingers and watched it spiral down into the depths.

Dave? She spun, losing the life jacket for a moment and frantically clawing at the water to get it back, then kicked her legs to rise up and looked all around. Dave and Rusty were both gone. Where?

Some 20 feet away, Steve bobbed quietly. She thought of swimming to him, but there was nothing she could do if he needed help.

It was the cold that would kill her, she knew. She tried to draw her knees up and wrapped her arms around her torso and the life jacket to conserve heat. She couldn't think what to do. Couldn't think. Her blood roared in her ears.

And after a long time there was a different roaring. She was barely conscious when they pulled her out.

••• — — — •••

Some 45 minutes passed before rescuers reached the site and pulled Shannon and Steve from the water. Both their radio and cell Mayday calls had been received but both were cut off before a location was heard. Helicopters and rescue craft immediately started a search, but without a location they were fighting long odds. In the dispatch center technicians rushed to work and were able to triangulate the brief cell call to narrow the search area. A fast Coast Guard vessel was first on the scene.

Shannon was hypothermic and almost incoherent, and it took a while to establish that there had been three people on the boat.

Steve was unresponsive. They administered CPR as the boat sped for shore, then turned him over to waiting EMTs who continued resuscitation efforts en route to the hospital, where he was pronounced dead.

A massive air and water search continued for Dave, with no luck. After a day the rescue mission became a recovery mission, but still with no luck. Eventually it was called off.

Two weeks later Rusty's body was found.

Almost a month later, police were called to a home along the shore where Dave's body had washed up.

The Coast Guard reminds all boaters to wear PFDs at all times, to file a float plan before going boating, to have and use appropriate safety and communication equipment, and not to depend on a cell phone.

Too Much Freeboard

The Etchells 22 is a fast 30-foot sailboat designed for racing, and it was sailing fast today in the Solent off the Isle of Wight with three sailing students aboard. They'd departed Cowes in the morning for a full day's sail, with a lunch break in Yarmouth, but had turned back early because Brenda, one of the students, was getting cold. The wind was stronger than forecast, the sea was about 10°C, and Ryan had already given his sailing jacket to Brenda, so he was happy enough to turn back.

Ryan and Sandra, the sailing academy instructors, followed close behind the Etchells in the fast chase boat, a 19-foot launch with a diesel inboard, occasionally pulling alongside to shout encouragement or instructions. Ryan was driving and doing most of the teaching, as Sandra, age 20, was new and seemed hesitant to say much. He wondered if she was as worried about the Swedish student as he was. Sandra had just started work Monday, 4 days ago, but surely she'd heard about the Swede's mishap last week.

No one knew quite what to make of the Swede. He was huge—over 1.8 meters tall and weighing over 120 kilograms—and was in his mid-forties. He was a nice enough guy and a good learner, but why would someone that big want to sail a small boat? He'd surprised them all when he'd arrived at the academy in Cowes a week ago to start the professional crew course, and the first thing they'd had to do was take him shopping for gear since none of the academy's waterproof clothing or life jackets fit him. Wouldn't you think a guy that size, who supposedly already had some sailing experience, would have his own gear?

Worse yet, the Swede moved slowly, not a good attribute for a sailor. He was like a big, friendly bear, Ryan thought.

So Ryan hadn't been thrilled to be assigned to the Swede's first sail last Saturday in one of the training dinghies. At least he made good ballast with all that body weight, but it was a tight fit with Ryan and him in the boat. After they'd sailed off the floating dock and he'd explained everything to the Swede, it seemed to take forever for the big man to trade positions with him to take the tiller. Then in their first tack the Swede moved the tiller so slowly that the boat stalled in irons into the wind.

On the second tack it happened. Ryan was handling the jib-sheets when the Swede muttered "Hard alee" and started to tack. He didn't quite see how the Swede had gotten tangled up in the mainsheet during the tack or how he'd managed to hook one of his legs over the tiller as the dinghy heeled over on the new tack, he just saw how the Swede, struggling to disentangle himself, half stood and then pitched overboard.

Thank god the chase boat was there in seconds. The Swede was unable to pull himself back on board the dinghy or the chase boat, so Ryan took the tiller and made sure the Swede hung on to the transom as the chase boat towed them some 90 meters back to the dock.

Later, the Swede laughed it off, but the instructors met and talked over the situation and decided to move him to one of the larger keelboats for the next steps of his training. And Ryan was happy now to be in the chase boat instead of in the sailboat with him.

Ryan turned to Sandra. "Since we're getting back early, we have to decide how to spend rest of the afternoon."

But Sandra was watching the Etchells and now pointed. "They're pretty much on a dead run," she said. "Should we have them jibe?"

The thought of it made Ryan nervous. The wind had gotten up some, closer now to Force 5 than the forecast 3 to 4, and the Etchells carried a big mainsail. "I think they better head up a little instead," he said, and slid the throttle forward a notch to ease up alongside.

The Etchells was on starboard tack, the sails well out to port. The Swede sat forward on the starboard deck tending the main-sheet. Brenda and Karl, the other two students, both slight of build, sat to port to counterbalance the Swede's weight on the run. Karl was at the helm, Brenda playing the port jibsheet.

"Turn about 20 degrees starboard!" Ryan shouted as they came up behind the sailboat. "Broad reach!" He watched as Karl carefully shifted over to the starboard side and made the turn.

None of the three seemed to be having a very good time, Ryan thought. Was it just the normal jitters, or were they actually a bit scared?

According to their applications, both Karl and Brenda had sailed some but it had been a few years ago for both. In the class-room they seemed knowledgeable and confident, but on their first outing 2 days ago, neither of them—nor the Swede—had done very well in the other keelboat. From the chase boat Ryan and another experienced instructor had watched while the three glided toward shore in a light breeze. "Time to tack!" he'd shouted, and they'd started the move okay but had released the jibsheet way too soon and were much too slow to tighten the main, and they blew it. Their second attempt was even worse. Worried they'd go aground before finally getting turned away from shore, Ryan had pulled up alongside and boarded the keelboat to take control.

Back to the classroom.

Today, however, after many more hours of instruction, they seemed reasonably in control. The Etchells held a straight course on a starboard broad reach and the sails were trimmed well.

"Time for a new helm," Sandra said to Ryan. "Brenda needs some tiller time."

"Right," he said, and began easing the launch closer to give them a shout.

An Etchells 22 is seldom used for beginning sail training for the same reasons it is an excellent race boat. The sleek hull and fin keel let it turn on a dime. Well ballasted, it is generally stable even in strong winds, but crew position is always important. The boom is low and long, providing for a large mainsail, but forcing crew to be nimble to duck below it on a tack or jibe. The cockpit is shallow but has room for the legs of three or four (average-size) crew. There are no stanchions or lifelines, and when close-hauled the crew sit on the windward rail hanging out over the water.

All of which means that a critical aspect of sailing an Etchells is the ability to move smoothly and quickly from one side of the boat to the other, ducking below the boom as it crosses while maintaining perfect control of the boat.

At the helm, Karl watched the launch approaching. Ryan shouted something. Karl cupped his free hand behind his ear, then turned and said something to Brenda, but she made an I-don't-know gesture. The Swede leaned back, apparently to listen.

As Ryan brought the launch closer and swung to starboard, Karl turned first to his left and then twisted all the way back and around to his right to watch the launch, inadvertently jerking the tiller behind him. The Etchells responded instantly by turning to port, swinging away from the launch where now both Ryan and Sandra were shouting, "Starboard!" Too late the crew realized they were jibing and Brenda and then Karl quickly leaned down just ahead of the boom snapping across the cockpit.

The Swede hadn't started to duck but instead had risen slightly as if to stand, and the boom swung into his ample belly and pushed him overboard.

Ryan reacted immediately and brought the launch near where the Swede, wearing a life jacket, floated in the chop. Sandra watched the Etchells moving away, now on a port tack with the mainsail out full and the jib backwinded, the students making ineffectual adjustments as they stared back at the launch. Oh, well, they'd either get it under control or they wouldn't, but at least the Etchells shouldn't capsize.

Ryan throttled down and slipped into neutral. "Are you okay?" he yelled to the Swede. "Are you hurt?"

"Okay," came his reply. "Just cold!"

Thinking of the launch's propeller, Ryan eased back into gear and idled up to the Swede, then cut the engine. At midships he knelt at the gunwale and leaned down and grasped the arm the Swede raised. "Okay, good. Now let's get you out of there."

Fortunately the launch was big and well balanced with the ballast of its diesel inboard, so they didn't have to worry about tipping or taking on water with the weight of all three of them on one side. But it had a freeboard of about 1 meter, making it impossible for the Swede to climb aboard by himself.

Sandra joined him at the rail. "Give me your other hand," she told the Swede. She took hold.

"On three," Ryan said, and they both pulled as they strained their leg muscles to stand with the Swede's weight.

His hands rose in the air above the rail, but they lost leverage as more of his body left the water and he grew heavier, and he slipped back into the water.

"Okay, again," Ryan said. "This time, grab the rail with your hands. Got that? You hold on so we can let go a moment and grab you down lower."

The Swede nodded. His teeth were chattering audibly and his eyes were rapidly moving around.

They pulled again and were able to get the Swede's hands on the rail. He curled his fingers and held on while Ryan leaned far over, feeling along the side of the Swede's torso for something to hold on to. Finally he just grabbed a handful of cloth and pulled. He had the lower part of the Swede's jacket, below his life jacket, and it rode up on him when he pulled—then nothing. Leaning over with almost no leverage, he couldn't raise him more than a few inches.

Sandra was frantically searching the launch, tossing aside fenders and coiled lines and kicking jerry cans. "There isn't a rope ladder? Why isn't there a rope ladder?"

Ryan knew why but didn't say it aloud; most of their students weighed less than the Swede and usually it would be faster to pull a person aboard than get a rope ladder and put it over the side. "Just get a heavy line," he called back over his shoulder, still holding on to the Swede. "Hurry!"

She uncoiled a dock line and threw one end over the rail beside Ryan.

"Hey!" he called to get the Swede to look at him. "Tie this around your waist."

The Swede stared at him. He had been in the water only a couple of minutes but he seemed to be losing touch already. But he took the end of the line in one hand and let go of the boat with the other, dropping back into the water. Ryan bent and reached down and held the collar of his life jacket to steady him as he fumbled with the rope underwater.

It took a long minute, but then the Swede raised both hands back up.

Ryan and Sandra grasped the rope and pulled. The Swede twisted in the water and then reached both hands back down. His life jacket rose up his torso, and they could see the rope had slid up his chest to his armpits. "Keep your elbows down!" Ryan shouted, and they pulled with all their might.

But his body rose no higher than it had before, and still they had no leverage. Ryan stepped back, braced both feet against the inner hull, and leaned back with all his weight, but it made no difference. His mind racing, he tried to think of anything from his training. On a sailboat they'd bring the boom over and above the victim and winch him straight up from the water, but nothing on the launch gave them height or leverage.

"I've got an idea," Sandra was saying. "We make a loop in another line for his foot and cleat it off when he steps into it. Maybe we can get him to stand up, work the line up. Or even one for each foot, tightening them alternately."

"Do it," Ryan said. When she released her hold on the first line to get another, he could no longer hold the Swede, who again slid down the hull.

Now the Swede was panicking, clawing at the hull with his hands, his mouth open and bubbling. He was fumbling with the line around his chest. "Leave it!" Ryan shouted at him, but the Swede suddenly raised both arms to reach for the rail and the loop slipped up and off his body. Ryan bent over and was able to grab one of his arms.

Sandra had tied a quick bowline loop and lowered it over the side. "Grab it!" she directed the Swede. "Get your foot in it, like a rope ladder."

The Swede seemed to stare at the loop but made no move for it, and they saw his eyes suddenly roll back and close and Ryan felt his heavy weight go limp. "Oh god, he's unconscious!" he said. Sandra briefly locked eyes with him, then she jerked away from the rail and ran to the helm.

A second later he heard her shouting Mayday into the radio. Three times, just like they were taught, then the name of the boat and the longitude and latitude from the GPS. "Man in the water! Can't get him aboard! We need help fast!" She repeated the longitude and latitude, then paused. The radio crackled back; the Coastguard had heard her. A few more quick questions while Ryan held the Swede as high as he could to keep his open mouth above the waves slapping the hull, and then the school's other fast boat broke in on the radio and said they were on their way too.

"I think he's stopped breathing!" she heard Ryan yell above the sound of the radio. "Gotta do rescue breathing."

Sandra made a last transmission to inform the Coastguard she had to get off to help the victim.

"Hold his arm," Ryan said when she reached him. "I'm going to lean way down so hang on to my belt."

With her left hand she held the Swede's arm as high as she could, and with her right she grabbed the waistband of Ryan's pants as he leaned over and eased down, getting as close to the Swede as he could. He had trained in rescue breathing from the side of a pool and on a low dock, but that had been a long time ago, and trying to do it from 1 meter away while hanging over the side of a boat was very different. After a moment he found and grasped the collar of the Swede's jacket below his throat with his left hand, then pinched his nose closed with his right. Another wiggle and he got closer and put his mouth over the Swede's and blew in, counting one long beat. Release. Repeat. With his abdomen pressed hard against the launch's rail, taking most of his weight as he leaned over, he could barely breathe himself. Release. Repeat. He had no idea whether the air was going in.

"Ryan," he heard Sandra say, "I can't hold you, my muscles are . . ." and he felt her grip slipping.

He pulled back. "It's okay. I'm going in." In a moment he was climbing over the rail in his life jacket.

A movement caught her eye and Sandra looked up. The Etchells! She'd forgotten all about them, but here they were at last, slowly tacking up to the launch. "Get over here!" she shouted. "We need your help!"

The students had apparently just drifted downwind a ways before taking control, and had had to tack back up to the launch. At least they seemed to know what they were doing, she found herself thinking, at least they're in trim. She quickly looked down at Ryan and saw him beside the Swede, giving in-water rescue breathing just like she'd been taught only a few months ago. Something she'd then been certain she'd never actually have to do.

Then she looked back at the Etchells. They'd come about to the other tack—good. She waved with her free arm and shouted, "Come around on our other side. Upwind side. Stall out and let the wind push you against us."

At the helm Brenda waved her understanding, and the Etchells shot past to make its turn upwind. Sandra wondered whether she dared let go of the Swede's arm long enough to help secure the Etchells to the launch and decided no, she had to help Ryan or else he and the Swede might float way. The students could do it on their own.

She watched over her shoulder as the Etchells turned as if to tack in order to go in irons and drift back, but Karl didn't get the mainsheet loose fast enough, it seemed jammed in the cleat, and she swore as the sailboat passed the launch on the other tack, jib flapping loose, being blown back downwind. Damn it all! Now they'd have to set the sails, make way, tack back, and try it all over again! And it was getting gustier.

Abruptly the radio crackled. "Powerboat northeast of Yarmouth. Powerboat a mile offshore east of Yarmouth. This is the fishing vessel *Agatha* a half mile astern. Do you require assistance?"

She craned her neck to look back over the stern and saw a small rusty trawler steaming toward them. She didn't dare release the Swede to go to the radio; why hadn't they tied him to a line? She tore her cap off her head and waved it frantically at the fishing boat. A glint of light, maybe binoculars. The vessel was coming closer.

Two minutes later the trawler was close enough for her to see a face in the wheelhouse window and another man on deck positioning fenders as the boat steered for their windward side. She saw the Etchells returning now on a tack toward the fishing boat and she waved them off. They were too far away to hear her, but she prayed they would realize it would be easier to pull the Swede up into the Etchells than the launch or the fishing boat and would come right back.

Then the trawler bumped once against the launch, lightly, and one of the men stepped off and into the launch. "He's not breathing," she explained hurriedly. "We can't get him back up."

The fisherman looked over, then immediately dropped the end of the line they'd used earlier back into the water. "Tie it around him," he said. "Let's pull him up."

For a moment Sandra felt hope—they'd finally get him out, help was on the way—but then realized it was just the two of them—she and the fisherman—because Ryan couldn't stop the rescue breathing long enough to climb back aboard to help. And even if he did, she doubted the three of them could do it; it was just too much weight with no leverage.

They tried their best nonetheless, the fisherman straining until the tendons in his neck seemed about to burst, but without success.

"Your boat," Sandra said, "you have winches, yes? Something like a boom we can swing over him to hoist?"

He looked at her, thought a moment, turned and looked at the trawler standing off some 30 meters to windward. "Yep," he said. He gestured at the radio. "That thing work?" She nodded. "I'll call the boss, then."

Sandra remembered the Etchells again and looked around to find it and wave them off again, get it out of the fishing boat's way. But as she raised her head to look, she heard the noise of an approaching helicopter.

Thank god.

The Coastguard was on the radio. The fisherman nodded at her and reached down for the Swede's arm. She dashed to the radio. It was the helicopter.

Then things happened very fast and she didn't have to think anymore but just do what they said. The helicopter hovered just to leeward, the downdraft from its blades whipping the water into froth, and a basket came down on a wire. The rescue swimmer was in the water already and quickly swam the basket over to the launch. Sandra and the fisherman helped steady the cables at each end of the basket while Ryan worked with the swimmer to maneuver the Swede into the basket. The last thing Sandra noticed was the look of surprise in the rescue swimmer's eyes as the cable was hoisted and he saw clearly for the first time the size of the victim.

Ryan was exhausted, but the fisherman got him back aboard with a jerk. He lay still a long moment, then sat up and started slapping his arms and legs to get his blood flowing. The helicopter was already gone.

A minute later the fisherman stepped over the rail back to the rear deck of the trawler and the boat moved away. She hadn't even had time to thank him.

"Where are our students?" Ryan said.

God, she thought, spinning around, and spotted them well to windward, on the other side of the trawler. They hadn't capsized, and she could see the two of them aboard.

The radio crackled again. It was the sailing school's other rescue boat, still coming on fast, now about a nautical mile away. "It was the Swede," Sandra explained. "They've got him in the helicopter."

She was glad they asked no more questions except "Anything we can do to help?"

She and Ryan looked at each other, and she reached for the ignition key. "Yes," she said, "the Etchells—can you take them back?"

"Roger that."

She started the engine and shifted into forward. The helicopter was almost out of sight now, flying fast and low over the water. There was a hospital just a few miles away in Cowes, no need to waste time now gaining altitude.

The helicopter crew started CPR as soon as the basket was inside the helicopter. The Swede's body felt very cold, but that didn't mean much, and could be to his advantage. As soon as they got his chest dry they attached the defibrillator pads, but there were no electrical signals from the heart. They kept up CPR until EMTs took over when they landed.

The emergency department staff took over at the hospital and made every effort to resuscitate the Swede, but less than an hour after he'd been removed from the water he was pronounced dead.

••• — — —•••

The foregoing is a retelling from the facts described by the UK's Marine Accident Investigation Branch (MAIB), which thoroughly investigated this incident. The pathologist who conducted the post-mortem examination of the Swedish sailor stated the cause of death was hypothermia. The MAIB investigation, however, concluded that death by hypothermia was unlikely after only 24 minutes in the water and suspected heart irregularities.

Investigators also carefully considered all actions, decisions, and the boats and equipment used by the sailing academy, including the background and experience of the students and instructors. No faults were found, and in normal circumstances survival could have been expected for at least 45 minutes or longer in the water, during which rescue by academy resources would have occurred. The only deficiency found was that they had not foreseen possible problems recovering a man of this victim's size from the water, particularly given the "high risk" of falling from the type of boat he was sailing on. The academy thereafter took new measures in its safety management program, and the MAIB made no further recommendations. The actions of the instructors were praised.

In the end, what we can learn from this incident, as in so many others, is the importance of constantly being prepared by questioning "what if" such a thing happens.

Briefly

The English Channel, May 2011. It wasn't stormy, but a west wind of about 25 knots had raised moderate seas in the channel. Aboard the 40-foot Beneteau were the skipper, mate, and eight paying crew, among them a relatively inexperienced woman in her early twenties. They were running downwind under a spinnaker when the sail tore. The mate and two crew rushed forward, lowered and gathered up the sail, and began to hoist a heavier spinnaker, which slipped out of control and wrapped around the forestay. Over the noise of the wind and the flapping sail those on the bow couldn't hear the skipper's shouted instructions, so he turned the helm over to the nearest crew, the young woman, and went forward himself. Minutes later she became worried about a fishing boat close ahead and shouted to the skipper for instructions, but she couldn't hear what he said. In the confusion she moved the helm slightly and the boat instantly jibed. As the main and boom swung across the cockpit, the mainsheet tackle smashed into her, sending her to the deck, unconscious and bleeding from a head wound. A rescue call was made, and she was evacuated by helicopter and then hospitalized with head and spinal injuries. The unlucky incident had occurred within seconds, but luckily she was not knocked into the water, although her injuries did require 2 months of hospitalization followed by physical therapy.

North Carolina, October 2010. The sailboat's owner was a member of the Coast Guard Auxiliary, an organization of experienced boaters whose mission includes teaching boating safety courses. He was sailing today with his wife and some friends, including another auxiliary member. It was a pleasant day and they were enjoying themselves when the boat jibed. Perhaps it was a sudden wind shift, or perhaps the bow was pushed over suddenly by a wave, or perhaps the person at the helm looked aside for a moment in conversation or to check the chart, for the skipper would not have been standing where he was if he had foreseen the risk. The mainsail slammed across the cockpit in the jibe, and the boom struck the skipper's head and knocked him overboard. Immediately a friend dived in to get the unconscious man, and they got him up into a nearby powerboat and rushed him to shore. A waiting Coast Guard boat transported him to medical care. Tragically, however, his injury proved fatal.

Columbia River, Oregon, October 2011. A solo sailor, age 81, had owned his Tartan 33 sailboat for only 4 weeks. He was on the broad Columbia River near Portland, an easy enough place to navigate if you pay attention to the chart, but he didn't have one on board. He should have, because he couldn't see deep enough into the water to spy the sandbars. Three or maybe four times already he'd felt that grinding shudder as the keel struck bottom, but at least it was sand and mud and the current pushed him right off and into deeper water. Then there was that railroad bridge ahead.

A swing bridge, it would open if he radioed to request it, assuming there wasn't a train coming, but it really looked high enough that he could get under it. He was so sure about that that he was shocked by the impact when his mast struck the bridge. The boat skewed around at an angle and heeled over as the current under the bridge pushed on the hull, but the mast was caught in the bridge structure. He had his life jacket on and was able to hold on. Water swirled over the coaming and partly filled the cockpit, some splashing down the companionway, and he had time to wonder if he'd live long enough to make it to shore if the boat filled and went down, but almost immediately he heard sirens. Soon a fireboat raced up and firefighters clambered aboard and were able to get him off without too much trouble. The boat—well, he didn't want to think about what the repairs were going to cost him. He felt lucky enough this time just to be alive. And next time, he'd make sure he had the right charts aboard.

CHAPTER 4

Anchoring, Docking, Dinghying

*M**any sailors who are safety conscious and take steps to stay safe when sailing tend to relax when the boat is near land or coming to a stop. It is as if we let down our guard because we no longer anticipate any risk. After all, shore's right there, and what could possibly go wrong now? Surprisingly, however, statistics show that collectively these situations are as dangerous as any other on the water—and perhaps more so if you let down your guard too far.*

Long Voyage, Quiet Harbor

Man, was he cold! Despite the balmy July evening air, he just couldn't get warm. Comes from 6 days at sea, he thought; his muscles just weren't moving enough to generate heat sufficient to combat the last 2 cold days after crossing the Gulf Stream into frigid New England waters. And he was tired, dead tired, deep to his bones.

From the cockpit of his 43-foot sloop swinging gently on a rented mooring, he looked across the quiet harbor to shore. Three kids at the water's edge were throwing bread crumbs to some ducks while seagulls screeched overhead in the dusk. In the light of a streetlamp just above the harbor, a couple paused in their stroll to kiss. For the hundredth time he missed his wife and kids, whom he hadn't seen since he'd sailed for Bermuda some three weeks ago. Their voices on his cell phone when he'd arrived just made him feel lonelier. Well, he'd be home soon enough. If he slept well tonight and the weather held, he'd leave tomorrow for the easy passage home.

He thought about just crawling into his sleeping bag in the quarter berth right now. But, as always, he felt the call of land after days at sea. He just wanted to walk a bit along the shore, stretch his cold, cramped legs. Warm up. Maybe find a pub nearby and have a beer, just one that he would sip slowly while listening to human sounds and shore life, gradually easing back into "normal" life. Hear what regular folks talked about instead of radio reports of weather, wind, and waves. He smiled; the sailor come ashore, such a stereotype—and so true!

But he delayed a little longer, feeling so at home in the cockpit that it was difficult to leave. He sat still a while, twirling an empty beer bottle in his hands. The token beer, the only one he brought back on the boat from Bermuda, carefully saved for the ritual of making landfall. With a grin he'd poured the first ounce overboard in thanks to Neptune, then had drunk the rest of it down, feeling it rush straight to his head, amazed it didn't put him straight to sleep. Six days of seldom more than an hour of sleep at a time, the single-handed sailor's plight. He hated running the engine just to power the batteries so he could run the radar to use its alarm function to alert him if a ship came too close. Better to use the timer to wake him every 20 minutes for a quick check of the horizon.

It wasn't as easy as when he was younger, but he was a long way from being old. At 48, he was looking forward to decades more sailing.

He looked at the shore again. The boys had vanished, the lovers had walked on. Lights were coming on in homes above the harbor. And only 60 yards away or so, there was a dock where he could tie up the dinghy and go ashore.

Rowing will help warm me up, he thought drowsily. Wake me up, too.

With one last look around the cockpit, he stood and wedged the beer bottle between two cushions where he could find it later to put below in the recycling bin. Everything looked shipshape.

His habit was to neaten things up on the approach into a harbor so he wouldn't have a mess to deal with later.

Knowing how fatigue would set in as soon as he slowed down, he'd pumped up the inflatable dinghy shortly after picking up the mooring, and it now bobbed on its painter just off the stern. He reached down the companionway and grabbed a flashlight for the row back to the boat later. Then he took out the hatchboards and the padlock from its hook on the aft bulkhead and secured the boat.

As he unclipped the swim ladder on the stern, he saw the ducks had now swum out to beg from him. He smiled again, remembering how his own kids when little had always wanted to feed the ducks and gulls.

He looked at the dinghy outboard mounted on the stern rail and thought it goofy to even think of using it; it was just a short row to the dock.

The ladder swung down and made a splash, sending the ducks scooting away. He shivered and was surprised again that he still felt cold. For the last 2 days he'd worn heavy wool pants and fleeces under his foul-weather gear, thick socks of Icelandic wool under his boots, and silk long underwear—a present from his wife—under all that, and had still been cold. Once moored, he'd stripped it all off and now wore only shorts and a T-shirt and the new hat he'd received as one of the race finishers, the better to soak up warmth from the air, but he still felt chilled.

Halfway down the swim ladder, pulling in the painter to bring the dinghy up to the hull, he paused and surveyed the cockpit again, an ingrained habit. It was part of staying safe out there, he'd lectured the kids; if you have to move fast all of a sudden you don't want to trip on a loose line. One of the too many lectures he'd given the kids, he reflected—like always wearing your life jacket and always clipping in with your tether when alone on a boat—and hoped that wasn't why none of them shared his passion for sailing. Like a religion, those safety rules had kept him safe while sailing, including the last 6 days alone on a big ocean.

All lines and halyards were neatly coiled and hung in place. She was a well-found ship, and he was proud of her. Everything was in its place.

Then he noticed his inflatable PFD crammed to one side under the dodger where he'd put it after securing the mooring pendant on a bow cleat. It was the one thing out of place, an aggravating detail. He should stow it away below, or better yet put it on for the dinghy ride. But shore was so close, the dock only 60 yards away, and he was tired. He let it be.

From the bottom rung of the ladder he swung the dinghy around with one foot and carefully stepped in. With his elbow crooked around the ladder, he coiled the painter and laid it forward out of the way, another longtime habit. Then he slipped the oars into the oarlocks and, after a final glance around, pushed away from the boat.

A bit of breeze had come up, ruffling the water's surface. It was colder right down next to the water. He rowed slowly, waiting for his muscles to start warming up.

When he was halfway to the dock, the ducks reappeared. He paused, and they swam right up to him, so close he shortened his starboard oar to avoid hitting one of them with his next stroke. The oar slipped in the oarlock when he moved it back in position, and when he leaned to his left to adjust it his new hat blew off into the water.

Gimme a break, he thought as he yanked the oar out of the lock and reached out for his hat. The breeze was moving the dinghy farther away from it and he almost put the oar back in the oarlock again to row to the hat, but it looked like it was starting to sink. He grabbed the oar at the end of the handle and leaned out.

He was in the water before he knew it.

It was so shockingly cold he didn't get his mouth closed, so cold his chest muscles spasmed and sucked in. It all happened so blindingly fast that he wasn't thinking at all as he went under.

The breeze pushed the dinghy slowly across the remaining distance to the dock, where it fetched up against a skiff tied up along the dock.

A short time later, another small boat brought a group of people up to the dock, where they found and secured an empty inflatable dinghy. Then they saw the body in the water and immediately radioed for help. The harbor patrol boat responded within minutes, but it was already much too late.

Late to the Slip

Just as Billy completed his turn down the row of finger piers and went into reverse, his cell phone rang. He couldn't hear it over the noise of the diesel, but he felt it vibrate in his pocket. Not a good time, he thought, and tried to ignore it. He was sure it was his wife wondering where he and Joe were and why they weren't on time— as he'd sworn they would be—for Joe's birthday dinner.

He glanced forward to the side deck where Joe was carrying back the bitter end of the cleated bow line, outside the lifelines. He figured Joe's cell would be ringing in about 10 seconds. Oh well. They'd call their wives back in about a minute once they got tied up.

He looked astern again as he backed toward the slip. The tide was running and the river had some current, but his new-to-him 36-foot sloop was backing smoothly under the little 13-hp diesel. No wind, so at least the bow wasn't blown sideways like last time.

No wind was also the reason they were late. The afternoon sail, a birthday day off work for Joe, had been leisurely and relaxed. At 46, Joe was several years younger than Billy, but they agreed about taking it easy on the water, accepting the light wind for what it was. So it had taken them longer than anticipated to get back in since Billy hated using the noisy engine and delayed starting it as long as he could. Way too long, he thought, checking his watch. It was after nine o'clock already, and the women were probably pretty aggravated.

This was his first time coming into the slip after dark, but the marina had good lighting and he had no trouble seeing what he was doing.

Joe had coiled the end of the bow dockline on the deck beside the starboard lifeline gate, just as Billy had asked. Now he stood with the stern line a few feet aft of the gate, ready to step down onto the dock.

The stern eased between the finger pier to starboard and the 36-footer tied up to port, the engine running slow as Billy went into neutral. He looked forward again to check that Joe was ready and saw him lift one leg over the lifeline. Joe had already taken off his bulky life jacket and tossed it on the cabin top near the mast.

The sailboat slid back through the dark water, quieter in neutral, and Billy heard Joe's cell ringing. They grinned at each other. "Don't answer it!" Billy called.

"Right. Just checking the caller ID."

Billy looked astern and darn it, they were still going a little too fast. He didn't like having to use forward gear to stop, since the prop walk pushed the stern to port. He was still looking back over his left shoulder as he engaged forward with a short noisy burst of power, belatedly swinging the wheel a quarter turn, hoping to compensate. He looked back again; still 10 feet to go before hitting the pier but slowing now. He threw the gear lever back into neutral, then rushed around the wheel pedestal and up out of the cockpit to take the bow line forward to tie off the boat. The boat was light enough that he could stop its motion with a cleat if needed.

At the gate he stooped and grabbed the line. Joe had already gotten off with the stern line, but . . .

He didn't see Joe anywhere. For a long couple of seconds Billy just stood there, stunned, wondering where Joe could have gone.

He snapped out of it only when the motion of the drifting boat caught his attention. He ran a few feet forward and quickly wrapped the dockline around a cleat.

"Joe?" It felt weird, like shouting to himself; there was nowhere Joe could be hiding. The shadows weren't that deep. He ran down the finger pier, part of his mind noticing the boat's stern swinging slowly farther out from the dock from the prop walk momentum.

Then he saw the aft dockline hanging down the hull from the starboard stern cleat, straight down into the dark water. The stern had slid out too far from the dock now for him to reach it, so he ran back amidships and grabbed a stanchion to pull the boat in. Then he worked his way back to the stern and grabbed the dockline and pulled.

It slid easily up and out of the water, and he realized he'd half expected a grinning Joe to emerge with it.

He looked all around. Except for the rumbling of the diesel the night was quiet, the water still but for the sliding ripples that showed a deeper current. Nothing anywhere.

Joe had to be in the water. But how? Where? He crouched down to scan all along the finger pier. Its smooth wood was the only interruption in the water's surface, not a sign, no one there— unless he'd somehow gone under?

Billy stood and raced up the pier to where it joined the main dock, then turned right and ran to where he could see the other side of his boat. Then he ran farther and checked both sides of the 36-footer, then checked again along the finger pier.

Oh god. Where else to look?

The phone in his pocket rang again. He jerked it out and saw his wife's name on the display. He hit the ignore key to send her to voicemail and punched in 911.

He never understood, later—not an hour later when the police divers brought up Joe's body, nor 2 days later after the postmortem was done—why he hadn't heard a splash. It was as if Joe had gone into the water like an expert diver without a ripple, had gone straight down without a struggle. They found a bruise on his forehead that might have come from hitting the dock or from striking the hull underwater. Worse, Billy was haunted by thoughts of the propeller, which Joe's shirt had been tangled on when the divers found him. He was certain he'd put the engine in neutral before Joe stepped off, he knew he had, and one of the divers told him later when he was sitting in the police car that the shirt wasn't actually twisted on the shaft, just caught on the prop, and the coroner did not find any slashes in the flesh, but could the prop have been turning nonetheless and caught him and held him down?

The transmission had been in neutral when he'd gone back aboard after making the 911 call to get the boathook to probe the water around the docks. He'd shut the engine down then. But he'd heard about props slowly spinning even in neutral if the clutch plates were too tight. He didn't know; he was still too new to this boat.

But what really bothered him was the thought that if he'd been watching and had seen Joe fall—or heard the splash—he could have gone after him. He could have brought him up before he drowned.

That thought, and wondering whether Joe would have kept his life jacket on a minute longer if he'd insisted, would haunt him forever.

The Season's Last Sail

Late-summer sailing can be a delicious treat in coastal New England. The crowds are gone, back to work and school, and the air is still tantalizingly warm. You can almost set your watch to the freshening southwest breeze, and when the halyards slap the masts, it's time to sail! There are days when you swear you are the only boat on the ocean and the late September slanting sunlight makes the tops of the waves sparkle like jewels. These truly can be the hazy, lazy days of late summer.

But late-summer sailing also has a bittersweet feel that can settle in your heart and bring on a tinge of sadness. After all, the weather won't hold forever and each sail could be the last of the season. Soon, maybe even tomorrow, it will be time to haul the boat, button it down, and spend the long New England winter reminiscing about the past season's adventures and planning next season's.

Maybe that's why this experienced sailor was a little preoccupied on this late September day. He and the first love of his life planned to spend the day on another love of his life—their 40-foot Bristol sloop—and end their sail where the boat would spend the next several months sleeping under a blanket of snow.

So much to do, so many details to take care of, but at least the weather was cooperating. The day dawned cloudless and warm, and the sky was the color of a robin's egg. "God," he thought to himself. "I love autumn in New England."

Even after more than 80 New England autumns, he still stood tall and strong. Muscular and weathered from a lifetime of sailing these waters, he could easily pass for a man 10 years younger. By all accounts, he was the perfect sailor: experienced, passionate, knowledgeable, patient, and perhaps most important, cautious.

"My father was the invincible iron man," his son wistfully reminisced a year later. "He wasn't careless or reckless. He thought things through. He was adventurous but cautious." His voice trailed off as he thought about what might have happened that fateful late September day.

The day started out just as hundreds, maybe thousands, of other sailing days had begun for the couple. The day before, they had completed their last cruise of the summer and picked up a mooring not far from their house, then relaxed on shore that night for the first time in several days. In the morning his wife drove them to the dock and dropped him off so he could take the dinghy out to their sloop and motor in to pick her up for the final day sail to the marina where the boat would be hauled out for the winter.

"Don't worry, honey, I'll be fine," she later remembered him saying. After all, he had done this hundreds, maybe thousands, of times before. It was really second nature for him: step down into the dinghy, give the priming bulb a couple of squeezes, set the choke, and start the outboard motor. When he was satisfied the motor was sufficiently warmed up, he'd cast off the painter and be on his way.

And, just like hundreds, maybe thousands of times before, he didn't bother to put on a life jacket.

"To be honest, my father never wore a life jacket in the dinghy," his son said later. "He was a strong swimmer, very athletic. Even well into his seventies, he would take off his shirt at the bow of the boat and just dive into the ocean and swim."

So today she parked the car and walked up to higher ground to get a better view of her husband and their boat. But even though she tried from different angles, she couldn't see the dinghy tied up to their sloop. She began to feel concerned but wasn't panicky; maybe the dink had drifted around to the side she couldn't see. But when she suddenly saw the empty dinghy drifting on the incoming tide up the harbor between other moored boats, she ran to a nearby house and called the local police.

"I suppose only the eyes from above truly know what happened that morning," his son recounted. "We'll never really know exactly how my father ended up in the water, but once he did, between the shock of what may have happened, the currents, and the water temperature . . ." and his voice trailed off again.

A search-and-rescue effort was mounted immediately, with the Coast Guard, state police, and environmental police joining in. The dinghy was found with the engine still running. Officers located his body not far up the harbor, where the tide had carried him.

What had started out as a perfect late-summer season-ending day of leisurely sailing ended tragically in an instant. As in so many unwitnessed accidents, no one truly knows what happened.

••• — — — •••

This narrative was contributed by Richard Joyce of Newburyport, Massachusetts, after several detailed conversations with the victim's son.

Briefly

Northern California, December 2010. The couple had completed their short voyage and were securely anchored before sunset, which came startlingly early as the winter solstice approached. The air temperature plummeted with the sun, so they went below for dinner and drinks. He sometimes drank more than usual after a day of sailing, and tonight perhaps even more because of the early dark and cold. Still, he took his boat responsibilities seriously and a little after eight o'clock he went back up on deck to check the anchor. Cleaning up in the galley, his wife paused the clatter of washing dishes to listen, then smiled as she heard the steady splash as he urinated over the rail. She went back to washing dishes and waited for him to come back. After a few minutes she called up the companionway, but there was no answer. She ran up the steps and stood on the cockpit seat to look over the dodger but he wasn't there; he wasn't anywhere. She went up to the bow and checked the water all around the boat—nothing. She yelled his name. She saw how the current was sweeping by the boat and realized he could be some distance away already, so she ran below and called in the emergency. Search boats, divers, and a helicopter arrived and searched all night, knowing he could not survive the 50°F water long without a life jacket, but unwilling to suspend the search too soon. By dawn, however, everyone had accepted the inevitable. He was gone, the fatal result of perhaps simply tripping over a line on deck.

Lake Michigan, north of Milwaukee, Wisconsin, October 2011. On a cool fall evening, the fisherman on the pier finished packing his gear and paused to watch a sailboat approaching the pier. It had slowed to a crawl, and the only sailor visible on board climbed out of the cockpit and made his way forward along the side deck carrying a coiled line. He looked to be about 60 and was moving somewhat unsteadily, which the fisherman first thought might be due to arthritis or an injury. He put down his tackle box to go over to take the man's dockline, if that was what was needed, but before he got close he saw the sailor try to throw a loop of the line over the top of a piling. He missed by some distance and fumbled when he started pulling it back in, and just as the fisherman realized the man was more likely intoxicated than injured, he saw the man lean out too far and fall into the water. He ran to the edge of the pier near where the man was flailing his arms. Others nearby were shouting, and he heard someone phoning for help as he reached down and was just able to grab the man's hand to keep his head above water. The sailor was not wearing a life jacket and was too heavy to pull out, even with the help of officers who arrived almost immediately. By then hypothermia had already set in and the sailor was a dead weight; they could only keep him high enough in the water so he could breathe. When the first diver in a dry suit arrived and jumped in the water beside the victim, even he couldn't get a harness safely around the man to hoist him out. Ultimately it took three divers in the water to get him out, and then he was rushed to the hospital. The sailor was lucky to survive. It all happened unexpectedly and so fast; if the fisherman had not been right there, if there had been even a minute's delay, the outcome could have been very different.

CHAPTER 5

Run Aground

*I*t is surprising to some that even in this day of inexpensive GPS units, boats still go aground on rocks, beaches, sandbars, reefs, and other shoal areas. But really, should this be any more surprising than the fact that boaters still drown in an age of inexpensive PFDs? As in most areas of boating safety, the issue is often that sailors who are not expecting a problem are less prepared to cope once it happens. As the stories in this chapter suggest, good seamanship is needed both to prevent grounding in the first place and to manage the situation if it does occur.

Tidal Estuary

This estuary area on England's east coast is notorious for its tidal shallows, and all three men on the sailboat knew they should be doing this crossing on a rising rather than a falling tide. But it had been a long voyage home from Spain, made even longer by earlier headwinds that had slowed their progress even under power. They'd planned to reach this area of shoals well ahead of high tide at 9 P.M., but it was after 3 A.M. and they still weren't through. They were too tired to hold off and wait for the next tide, though, so they watched the water and kept their fingers crossed.

Sadly, negatives always seemed to happen in multiples. They were late, they were tired, and visibility was poor. One crew watched forward into the fog, one studied the radar, and the helmsman followed the route they'd programmed in long ago on the tiny chartplotter.

Another problem was that their vector chart for this area was set to the wrong scale. And someone had forgotten to bring a large-scale paper chart to consult for better detail.

So they were more aggravated than surprised when the keel struck mud and the boat shuddered to a stop. It was a soft ground-ing, and fortunately no one was thrown forward and hurt. They assumed the keel was not damaged, at least not seriously. They were in no imminent danger and had time to talk over the best plan of action.

The main problem was that the tide was still falling and would be for an hour and a half. If they didn't get free very soon, the boat would lie over to one side, possibly bringing water aboard, and worse, they'd be delayed by hours more.

The skipper shifted to reverse and revved the engine. The prop spun furiously but the boat didn't budge. They conferred briefly, then moved the boom far out to one side and put the weight of both crew on it to heel the boat and thus shorten its draft and hopefully break free. Again he gunned the engine, but they remained stuck.

So they talked again. The 11-meter sailboat's draft was 1.4 meters, and they figured the water now was only about 1.2 meters deep. The last option was to carry the smaller Danforth anchor back to deeper water and try to kedge off with a winch. It seemed a good plan, but it would take too much time to pump up the inflatable dinghy. So the skipper reluctantly volunteered to carry out the anchor, tied a long line around his waist, and slipped off the starboard aft quarter into the cold water. "Keep it hard in reverse," he called back. "Maybe she'll break free still."

One of the crew went to the helm and operated the throttle while the other paid out some line and readied the anchor to lower it to the skipper, who was standing chest deep in the water beside the boat.

It happened so fast that at first they weren't sure what was going on. One moment they were looking at the skipper in the water and the next he was gone. They tried to locate him with a flashlight but without success. Then they saw that the line he'd tied around his waist was pulled down along the hull and under the boat. "Neutral!" shouted the one at the rail. He yanked hard on the line, but it was taut as a bar down into the black water. The skipper had somehow been pulled beneath the boat.

"Kill the engine!" he shouted. Checking that his knife was still on his belt, he climbed over the rail and jumped in the water. He seized the line and felt down along it as far as he could, then he filled his lungs and ducked under, pulling himself down into the dark.

The water was totally black and shockingly cold. The tidal current surging past threw off his equilibrium, and it seemed to take minutes to pull himself down the line. He struggled on, and then his fingers touched the cold steel of the prop shaft and found that the line was tightly wrapped around it. But where was the skipper? Then he realized that a free loop in the line had caught on the prop, twisting in both sections of line along the shaft, and he let the current pull him farther aft along the shaft.

The skipper was still struggling, but only weakly, when his friend's fingers touched his sodden clothes. Frantically the friend tried to find the rope where it was tied around the skipper's waist. Then his lungs were bursting and he had to go back up for air.

Down again, following the line, not as disoriented this time, and he quickly reached the skipper. The skipper's body jerked once at his friend's touch, then stilled. Where was the damn line wrapped around him? He fought the current, feeling in the dark along the skipper's body with one hand while holding on to the prop shaft with the other, and then had to surface again for air.

On the third attempt he found the rope around the skipper's waist, but it cut so deeply into the skipper's flesh that he couldn't get a finger between it and the skin to be able to work the knife blade in. The rope was cinched tight against his ribs. Finally he clawed a finger beneath it, but before he could reach for his knife with his other hand he ran out of air again and had to surface.

Now he knew he had to cut the rope no matter what, even if he sliced up the skipper at the same time.

He was exhausted, the cold water sapping his strength as he went down for the fourth time. He had no idea how much time had passed—seconds or minutes or more—but he was going to get him free now at any cost.

This time he found the rope quickly and with brute force he shoved two fingers between it and the skin, held on, and sawed at the line as hard as he could.

It gave. Freed, they were both caught by the current and swept back as he struggled to stand in the mud. He shouted the moment his face broke the surface, and the beam of the flashlight held by the crewman on board found them immediately some 3 meters off the stern. As he worked to pull the skipper's motionless body above the surface and back toward the boat against the current, the crew on board threw him a line and helped pull them both back to the stern.

They couldn't remember later how exactly they got the skipper back on the boat; probably with a great heave and an adrenaline rush. One of them had taken a CPR course once and did his best to resuscitate the unconscious skipper.

The crew who had remained on the boat had made a Mayday call on the radio. While they were still pumping the skipper's chest, the first lifeboat and then a helicopter reached them. In minutes the experts took over CPR and then hoisted the skipper to the helicopter, which departed immediately for a hospital.

The two crew went aboard the lifeboat after a second rescue boat arrived, and arranged to put a towline on the stricken sailboat to tow it in when the tide rose.

Shortly after they reached shore in the lifeboat, they learned the skipper had been pronounced dead at the hospital.

On the Rocks

The mouth of the Merrimack River in northeast Massachusetts is one of the most dangerous boating areas on the East Coast. With a tidal flow that extends for several miles back from the Atlantic, the Merrimack also brings water down from far up in New Hampshire, and its current is typically 3 knots or more on the flood tide and considerably faster after heavy rainfall upstream. Along the way the river picks up silt and sand and then funnels between two breakwaters extending a short distance into the ocean. Where the current slows as the river blends into the sea, sand is deposited on a bar that rises abruptly from a depth of 30 feet to only 8 to 9 feet at low tide. When the wind is east on a hard ebb tide, steep breakers form and make the river mouth impossible for small boats to navigate and dangerous for large ones.

Fortunately, a hard east wind is rare, although the water is often choppy on the tide. Added to this, especially on summer weekends, dozens of small fishing boats hover between the jetties or just outside and larger craft throw big wakes as they zoom in and out of the river. For the uninitiated the mouth can seem a hellish maw, and the locals know when to keep away. Reportedly, on average two boaters die there every year, typically fishermen on small skiffs overturned by a wave or a wake, and sometimes crew from a larger boat that broaches in the breakers and capsizes or is bashed against the granite blocks of the breakwaters. One year a powerboat captain lost his life after hitting the jetty.

On the flood tide the current reverses at the mouth, usually flattening the waves and easing speeding boats' return voyages to ports upriver. Then it's mostly a matter of paying attention to the markers, staying in the channel, and avoiding other boats. A few intrepid sailors even come in under sail, occasionally tangling with powerboaters who seem to understand neither the rules of right-of-way nor why a sailboat must sometimes tack diagonally across the channel. On busy weekends only the bravest sailors thread this gauntlet under sail.

Once between the jetties, headed in, the channel bears hard to starboard around a sandbar extending from Plum Island, on the port side, more than two-thirds of the way across the water. It's clearly marked on the chart—the big green buoy with a flasher is obvious—and few boats risk cutting the corner below half tide. Yet

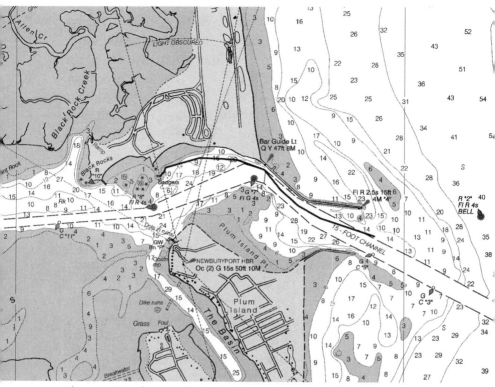

Chart section showing the track of the sailboat into the rocks.

fishermen and beachgoers wading out on this sandbar sometimes get in trouble when the water rises fast behind them, and recently a young woman was washed off by the current and drowned.

This Saturday afternoon was a typical summer weekend— sunny, a light southwest breeze, the river full of boats. Joanna and Seth were happy to have their three children with them for the day's sail. One had driven up from Boston, and the other two were home for the summer from college. The family of five filled the cockpit of the 28-foot sloop to capacity, but they were a close family and having a great time. Joanna especially was pleased by how well the kids still got along, and for his part Seth was thrilled they still wanted to go sailing. So many friends complained that their children had lost interest.

Not only that, but they helped with the sailing, too. The oldest boy had taken the helm while Seth and the younger boy dropped and furled the main in preparation for motoring in.

The boys then decided to drop a fishing lure in the water and troll during the ride up the river. With so many fishing boats around they figured the stripers must be running. Seth took the helm and steered to skirt the shore to starboard and keep away from most of the fishing boats.

The flood tide was running hard, and though the knotmeter showed only 5 knots under diesel power, Seth knew they were probably doing at least 8 over the bottom. But to the powerboats zipping by to port, they must have looked like they were standing still.

Past the flasher at the inner end of the breakwater, he eased still more to starboard, watching sunbathers on the beach and listening to the chatter of the boys leaning over the stern rail with the fishing pole. There were no markers here, and deep water held almost up to the beach. A couple hundred yards along you had to turn almost 90 degrees to port, across the river, to leave the red flasher to starboard.

Just as he started the turn to port, the boys shouted that they had a fish. "Feels huge!" Immediately Seth throttled down to ease the strain on the line. He looked back and saw the pole's tip bent down toward the water.

He turned more to port to make for the red marker since the incoming tide swept you sideways at this point. Then he turned farther to port so the boat was facing directly across the river.

When they struck the rocks he was so surprised that at first he thought a boat had hit them on the starboard side, but there was nothing there. Alarmed, he turned hard to port and throttled up to head back toward the center of the channel. The keel hit again, harder, and the boat heeled suddenly hard to starboard as the current pushed against the port side. With a shudder, the engine died when the prop hit a jutting rock.

"Everyone hang on!" he shouted.

The boat stopped, heeled even more, and then with a grinding noise slid farther into the rocks 3 feet under the surface. It was now canted over more than 30 degrees.

When he was sure they had stopped, at least for the moment, Seth dashed below to check for leaks. Once in the cabin he heard the steady grinding of fiberglass against granite and could only hope it was the keel and not the hull.

The tide was rising fast and might float them off, but he realized that the current would just push them deeper into the rocks. Things would only get worse.

He rushed back up to the cockpit where everyone waited, Joanna white-faced. "I'm calling the harbor patrol," he said. "We gotta get out of here." He handed out PFDs from the cockpit locker.

••• — — — •••

Fortunately the local Coast Guard crew heard their radio call and responded within minutes in a rigid-hull inflatable rescue boat that could work in close enough to take them off. Later, back at the station after Seth had called a salvage company to try to retrieve their sailboat, one of the guardsmen took Seth aside. "I don't want to scare your family, but you're really lucky you didn't end up in the water. It's still damn cold, and you'd have been bashed around in that current or on the rocks where a boat couldn't get to you." Seth nodded grimly. "And next time you might want to put your life jackets on before you need them. You never know."

The Reef of New South Wales

The Flinders Islet Race follows a 92–nautical mile course over mostly open ocean off New South Wales, Australia. While this race lacks the treacherous reputation of the Sydney–Hobart race, it nonetheless commands the attention of participating sailors. The forecast for the race in October 2009 was nothing special. Earlier strong winds had abated, leaving a big swell, and race winds were forecast to be 20 to 25 knots and subsiding. Experienced racers like Andrew Short weren't concerned about the weather but were looking forward to a fast, fun race.

Andrew had a crew of 17 aboard his 80-footer named *Price-WaterhouseCoopers*. He sailed often and knew the boat well. His friend Matt acted partly as tactician, and more than half of the others were regular crew on the boat. Some had sailed with him for over two decades on other boats. Others, like his friend Sally, were experienced sailors but new to this boat. All of them had gotten used to Andrew's style of sailing, however.

He liked to be in control, even though he was more relaxed than dictatorial in his command. He generally kept the helm for himself and also made the navigational and most tactical decisions. Unlike most other skippers he didn't plan out a rotation of crew roles in advance. After all, he likely reasoned before the race, it's only 92 miles, not a multiday race where you need to set watch schedules for sleeping.

So he took the helm as usual well before the start, late Friday, after a day's work. The adrenaline was flowing, and the crew was as happy as they could be in this weather. Everyone had full confidence in him as the skipper. They made a good run on the starting line and headed off downwind for Flinders under spinnaker. The southwest breeze was moderate at the start, but they had a reef in the main because they anticipated more wind offshore.

The evening weather became unpleasantly cold after passing showers. The wind averaged about 20 knots but gusted near 30, with frequent shifts in direction. Waves a meter high built on top of the swell from yesterday's gale. Some of the crew were feeling queasy by midnight.

A little before 2 A.M. they tacked onto port when the chartplotter showed they were about 6 miles from Flinders Islet. The plotter had been acting up earlier, but after they rebooted the system things seemed okay, and Andrew felt he could trust it now. The wind was still shifting, but he anticipated no problems in leaving Flinders to port, as required in the race, without having to tack again. He had been on the helm for about 7 hours now and was a little tired, but the weather was clearing and they were cheered by the prospect of a more pleasant return sail back to Sydney.

The moon came out as they approached the islet from the southeast, steering approximately for its northern end some 3 miles off. Andrew had overstood the mark with the earlier tack in case of a wind shift but could now fall off some to starboard. The boat was humming along at 12 to 15 knots as the crew readied the spinnaker lines for a quick hoist after they rounded the islet. The spinnaker bag was positioned on the port rail—the high, windward side—in preparation. The bag obscured Andrew's view forward from the cockpit on that side, but he was using the chartplotter more than line of sight as he steered to the mark.

PriceWaterhouseCoopers, like many large race boats, had two wheels, and Andrew was mostly using the high, port wheel. The plotter was closer to the starboard wheel, however, so he kept moving back and forth, sometimes switching to the starboard wheel to check the view to leeward, although the headsail blocked most of the view forward from that position.

Matt was just forward of the mast, readying the spinnaker pole and control lines.

Andrew drove on, closing the mark, unwilling to lose ground by bearing off any more than necessary. He shouted commands to the trimmers but had not asked or assigned anyone to be forward lookout. His crew was used to that; Andrew never lacked confidence in his helming or tactical decisions.

The sky was clear as they approached the last mile. Flinders Islet was now an obvious silhouette against the shore lights of Port Kembla in the distance. Everyone was in position for the rounding.

The boat flew off a swell and was surfing fast when Matt suddenly heard breakers. He spun around and saw they were sailing straight at the waves breaking on the rocks of the islet's north end. "Come away!" he shouted—and kept shouting—and Andrew turned to starboard.

Matt was still shouting. Andrew turned more.

Then they struck.

The crew described it later like a car crash, an instant full stop that threw them forward on deck, gear flying everywhere. Matt had been tethered to a jackstay and was thrown from the mast to the forestay, where his tether held him.

A quick check showed that everyone was still aboard with nothing more than minor injuries. Miraculously the boat remained upright on the reef about 10 meters from the exposed rocks of the shore. Quickly they released the sheets to spill wind from the sails, hoping to steady the boat.

But breaking waves continued to slam the boat forward and it slid around to point straight at the islet, pitching fore and aft with the waves.

Almost immediately after striking Andrew had ordered the engine started with the hope of backing off the reef. It ran for 30 seconds, died, and would not restart.

Still at the port wheel, Andrew then directed someone to make a Mayday call, but abruptly the boat lost all electrical power. Crew reported the cabin was a mess down below, with gear and sails tossed everywhere in the dark and breaking waves flooding in.

Somewhere down below, buried out of sight in the mess, were soft-pack life rafts. But someone did manage to find some flares.

Alone at the wheel, Andrew tried to get a handheld VHF radio to work but it also failed.

The waves kept pounding the boat, rolling it wildly, the boom swinging crazily side to side. Then the mast broke and fell over to port, luckily missing all crew. The hull pounded the rocks, the rudder broke off, and solid walls of water broke over the boat as it rolled violently on each wave.

Sally and some crew were tethered in, others were not, but almost none of them could hold on in one place as the waves swept them about the cockpit. Often they went underwater as a wave swept over the boat, struggling to breathe after it passed during the brief moments of calm.

No one had any time to make a plan.

Another big wave jolted by, and when it was past, Andrew saw that Sally had been swept through the lifelines on the port side. Her tether was still connected to the port jackline, but she was overboard. Matt and another crew tried to pull her back on board with the tether, but in the turmoil of water they were unable to move her. They saw she was unconscious, going underwater when the boat rolled.

"Big wave!" someone shouted. As it struck and the boat rolled, Matt and another crew were thrown across to the starboard side. The wave slammed Andrew into the port wheel and carried both him and the wheel with the pedestal overboard. He'd never had a chance to put on his PFD or harness.

The big wave lifted the boat and drove it higher onto the rocks in the surging surf and breaking waves. The crew saw they now had an opportunity—and probably a very short window of opportunity—to get off the boat and reach higher ground before the boat broke up.

As a group they jumped between waves and clawed up the rocks out of the surf. They couldn't see Andrew anywhere in the water. Some wanted to go back for Sally in case she was still alive, but when they moved to where they could see the boat's port side between waves, they could not see her. Her body was apparently underwater or had been washed away. The boat was breaking up, and they all realized the danger of even attempting to return to it.

Someone did a head count, and they discovered that in addition to Sally and Andrew, another crew, Nicholas, was also missing. The 15 of them gathered together on the islet. No one had a handheld VHF or even a cell phone. But they had some flares, and two crew activated their PLBs. They began firing off aerial flares at 2:42 A.M.

Because several other sailboats in the race were nearby, a search began almost immediately. Several boats spotted the flares and approached the islet, saw the wrecked boat, and began searching through the debris field nearby. Soon it was established that three people were missing, and it wasn't long before another sailboat found Nicholas floating alive in his PFD. Shortly after, Andrew's body was found, with signs of a head injury that may have knocked him unconscious before he drowned. Another sailboat found Sally floating facedown, no longer wearing her PFD or harness and also with an apparent head injury. That crew gave her CPR until she was transferred to a medical crew 30 minutes later, but she was unresponsive and was pronounced dead.

$$\bullet\bullet\bullet - - - \bullet\bullet\bullet$$

The Cruising Yacht Club of Australia's (CYCA) investigation of the incident focused on factors related to the yacht's fatal grounding but found no single reason or cause. Several contributing factors were cited, however. Although the GPS chartplotter may have shown location inaccuracies, the most important failing was overreliance on the plotter to the extent that no one was on lookout, even at a time when conditions allowed a perfectly clear view of the island ahead. With 18 persons aboard, someone easily could have been forward with a clear view. The fact that no one was on watch, the investigators concluded, was largely due to the skipper's loose organizational approach. In addition, fatigue—the skipper's 7 hours on the helm— was cited as a likely factor in navigational judgments made during the last minutes before the grounding.

Briefly

Northern California, November 2011. One of the big issues for long-distance solo sailors, of course, is getting enough sleep. Offshore and far from shipping lanes, with the right equipment and good weather, it's manageable, but this sailor had been struggling with gales for the last 2 days of his voyage from Hawaii to California. He'd made this voyage several times before, however, and knew what he was doing. Finally the weather eased, and the exhausted sailor checked the steering wind vane, set his alarm to wake him long before approaching shore, and lay down for a nap. Sometime later he woke to a brutal pounding as his boat was rocked and slammed down by surf off a beach. With the high, crashing waves it was not safe to try to get off the boat. His VHF radio was on the fritz, but his cell phone had a signal so he called his wife, who called the Coast Guard. The helicopter reached him quickly but was unable to drop a cable because the boat's mast was thrashing about, so they lowered a rescue swimmer nearby to help him off. Over the loudspeaker they told him to stay on the boat, but he sensed time was running out and leaped into the surf just before a big wave struck the boat, which snapped the mast, stove in the portlights, and filled the cabin with water. "Unlucky to sleep through the alarm," he told friends later, and, repeating what the rescue swimmer had said to him, "Lucky to have gotten off alive."

Coronado Islands, Mexico, April 2012. Four friends ranging in age from 49 to 64 were participating in the Newport to Ensenada race in a 37-foot sailboat. Like the other boats in the race, their position was being tracked by the boat's satellite transponder. Friday's sail was on a light but steady breeze, but after dark the wind died and they turned on the motor, accepting the race penalty for using the engine. The boat most likely was being steered by the autopilot. Around 1:30 A.M. Saturday, their tracking signal disappeared. Since no distress call or other communication had been received, race officials assumed it was a transponder failure. About 10 A.M., however, other boats passing through the area off the Coronado Islands started reporting boat debris in the water and the U.S. Coast Guard began a search. Many pieces of the boat were found, including a section of the transom with the boat's name on it. Then, as the search continued, they found three bodies in succession, all battered, none wearing a PFD. They continued searching for the fourth man and found more pieces of the boat, all fairly small and suggesting a violent collision. Sailors on other boats reported seeing a large ship in the area that night and speculation was rife that a ship must have run them over, but why hadn't they seen it? No calls had been made, no apparent evasive action had been taken, and they hadn't even put on their PFDs.

The Coast Guard reported the night had been clear, lit by a half moon, and sea conditions were calm. No one wanted to speculate aloud that the four men—all experienced sailors—might have been in the cabin below with no one standing watch. On Sunday evening the Coast Guard suspended its search for the fourth man. The coroner ruled that two of the three victims had died of blunt-force trauma, reviving the speculation that they had been run over by a large, fast ship. None of the boat debris suggested any other cause such as an explosion.

Then, 2 days later, the boat's GPS transponder track became available and it showed a straight-line course directly into the sheer cliff face of North Coronado Island. The pounding of the boat into the rocks over and over likely resulted in the small pieces of debris, which were then carried away by the current. While some still speculated that the boat might have been run over by a ship and then the transponder floated on and reached the island, it seemed obvious that the boat, motoring at 6 knots, had slammed into the cliff while no one was on lookout. Were they all below, or had a crew on watch in the cockpit fallen asleep?

Six days later the body of the fourth sailor was found washed up on the island not far from the suspected crash site. Later investigation revealed that the emergency button on the SPOT satellite messenger device had actually been activated, but because a GPS position was not transmitted along with the emergency signal, the emergency was not relayed to search-and-rescue authorities, a protocol flaw that was subsequently corrected. The GPS location may not have transmitted if the unit was in the water at the time.

CHAPTER 6

Engine or Equipment Failure

*A*nyone who has owned a boat for very long knows that things break down—often, and usually at the worst time. The water is a harsh environment, and the stresses and battering of wind and waves can knock almost anything out of commission. The engine may fail when you most need it, the chartplotter may die in a tricky channel, and the electrical system may give up and bring down instruments and communication equipment, to say nothing of sails or lines tearing or jamming or otherwise becoming inoperable. Experienced mariners say to expect such failures at any time; you should do your best to prevent them but be ready to act quickly when a breakdown leads to a situation that can threaten your safety.

The Delivery Skipper

Jonathan, who was in his early forties, was excited to be embarking on his first sailboat delivery despite the cold March weather in the English Channel. Maybe the weather was why the boat brokerage had hired him for the job, since they likely had more experienced regulars, or maybe it was just that his beginner's fee was lower, but in any case he was pleased to have landed the job. He'd worked hard to earn all his captain's certificates and commercial endorsements, and this was the beginning of what he hoped would become his new career.

The voyage itself, despite the weather, was simple enough—a one- or two-day trip from Southampton to Plymouth. He knew the Solent and the Channel well and anticipated no problems. The 9-meter sloop *Pastime*, built in Sweden in 1990, sounded like a well-equipped cruiser, and he'd had plenty of experience on boats of its size.

Jonathan's only apprehension as he packed his gear bag Friday morning was about dealing with his crew. Carlyle, the boat's new owner, was a decade older than he, and had said he knew how to sail but needed a refresher because he'd been away from boating for quite a while. Jonathan understood many of his future clients would be on board during the delivery cruise, but he'd heard that owners sometimes challenged the delivery captain or made poor decisions. There can be only one captain on a boat, and Jonathan didn't like arguing.

As soon as they met at the boatyard Friday morning, however, he relaxed. Carlyle seemed like a good egg who wouldn't cause any trouble, and he clearly accepted Jonathan's expertise and role as captain. They'd get along fine for a couple days, he was sure.

The boat, on the other hand, was more problematic than he had anticipated. First, the marina was late in launching it, making the owner worry about their schedule. Then the engine wouldn't start and it took some time before the boatyard mechanic managed to get it running. When it was finally running, they motored to the fuel dock and filled the tank, but it took several attempts to dock back at the marina because the wind was blowing hard off the dock. Finally they got it tied up and set about getting familiar with the gear. Jonathan asked to see the owner's pre-purchase survey of the boat and was a little dismayed to see the survey was only structural and hadn't tested the engine and systems.

At last they were ready to depart midafternoon. Given the delay and the later tide change at the Needles channel at the Solent's west end, they decided to motorsail to make better time. The forecast called for east and northeast winds of Force 5 to 7, so they started out with only a small jib and the engine, headed downwind down the Solent.

With the tidal current, engine, and wind at their back, they flew southwest at a speed over the bottom that the GPS clocked at almost 10 knots. It was cold—the water temperature was only 7°C—but at least they stayed dry in the cockpit. And the boat managed the rising seas well. Jonathan was happy enough to let Carlyle do most of the helming through the afternoon.

Before sunset they discussed a watch schedule for the night. Once they were out of the relatively sheltered Solent in the higher seas of the English Channel, they both admitted to feeling queasy whenever they went below in the cabin, so they decided they'd both stay in the cockpit and take turns trying to sleep there. The wind was still rising and the seas were growing, so Jonathan suggested that Carlyle tether himself in with his harness and safety line. Jonathan's own harness and tether were still in his gear bag, but he wore his life jacket at all times in the cockpit.

Then the engine's overheating alarm went off. Damn, Jonathan thought, there should've been an engine survey. At least they were a long way from being becalmed, although if the wind rose much more, they'd be caught in a gale sweeping the Channel. They shut off the engine and sailed on under the jib.

Thirty minutes later a pin fell out of the mainsheet traveler assembly and the boom started swinging wildly. Luckily they were able to control it quickly since the mainsail wasn't up.

A little later the port and starboard running lights blinked off after a big wave crashed over the bow. Then all the cabin lights went off. Jonathan gritted his teeth against his queasiness and went below to work on the electrical panel, holding a flashlight between his teeth. Finally he was able to get power flowing again.

All was well for a couple hours, and then the power failed again. All the lights and instruments went down, including the GPS. This time, no matter what he tried, Jonathan couldn't get electricity flowing again. They did have a backup handheld GPS unit, but it inexplicably failed to lock onto a position.

It was almost 11 P.M., and both men were exhausted, particularly Carlyle, who had done most of the steering. Jonathan took over the helm. It was tiring work, as the seas had grown and were knocking the boat about.

They were still sailing downwind on a starboard tack under just the jib, and sometimes Jonathan had trouble avoiding a broach when a wave or gust knocked the bow over. They were both seated on the low, port side, Carlyle hunkered down in the aft corner trying to sleep, Jonathan beside and just forward of him. Whenever the bow was pushed to starboard, the boat heeled dramatically and Jonathan had to force the tiller away hard to correct their course. He had become very weary.

At one point he realized he should probably be tethered in. But Carlyle had finally gotten to sleep, and he didn't want to wake him to take the tiller so that Jonathan could go below for his harness and safety line.

Then a large wave struck and again the boat headed up and heeled sharply. Struggling to shove over the tiller to prevent a broach, Jonathan leaned forward and half rose from the cockpit seat. Abruptly the boat righted, pitching him forward off balance. As he crouched, struggling to regain his balance and footing, another wave heeled them to port and he fell backward and was pitched out of the cockpit over the rail, striking Carlyle's head with his knee as he went overboard.

Carlyle woke to Jonathan's shout as he was toppling, but the sudden blow to his head knocked him out for a few seconds.

When he came to, Carlyle saw he was alone in the cockpit. He was wet all over and his PFD had inflated. In a panic he looked back at the water and saw a light in the darkness some 40 meters back; could that be the light on Jonathan's life jacket?

He reacted quickly and grabbed the horseshoe buoy from its rail mount and threw it in the direction of the light in the water. He swung the tiller and started winching in the jibsheet as he turned the boat back toward the wind. He soon realized it was hopeless, however; with just the small jib and the high wind and waves, it

Pastime *at the time of recovery the day after the incident. (Courtesy of MAIB)*

would take forever to claw his way back upwind toward Jonathan's position. He'd lost sight of the light already and couldn't mark his position without the GPS.

He went to start the engine, hoping to be able to motor back into the wind, but the engine wouldn't turn over. Probably not enough juice left in the batteries to power the starter.

But there was enough power for the VHF radio, which still seemed to be working, and he was able to reach the Portland Coastguard station with a Mayday call. Without the GPS, however, and not knowing how far they'd come since their last known position, he was not able to estimate their current position.

Carlyle was able to make four brief transmissions before the batteries failed. He gave what information he could about their course and what time they'd passed the Needles, but when the radio went silent he didn't know what the Coastguard would be able to do.

Now he could only wait and try to stay roughly in the same area, tacking back and forth but making little headway upwind, straining his eyes into the darkness in the hope of seeing Jonathan's light.

The Coastguard, meanwhile, had been able to triangulate an approximate position from his radio signals and the course data he'd provided. They put out an all-ships bulletin, and five merchant ships responded and began searching. Lifeboats were launched from multiple locations, and a SAR helicopter took off.

Carlyle didn't know a search had begun, but he was planning to carefully shoot off a series of flares, hoping someone would be close enough to see them. He had a number of handheld red parachute flares, which he was going to use at intervals of 20 minutes. Without good light and with his reading glasses down below, he couldn't read the instructions printed on the flares, however. He couldn't ignite two of the flares at all, and a third burned his hand badly when it went off. But he did manage to fire off the others, one of which was seen by the helicopter as it approached the area.

It was after 1:30 A.M. when the helicopter sighted the boat and started a search pattern upwind of it after radioing the position to the lifeboats. Ten minutes later the first lifeboat reached the sailboat. Its crew immediately took Carlyle off, who was suffering from exhaustion and shock, and set out for shore.

Time was everyone's concern. It was now 2 hours since Jonathan had gone into the cold water, a dangerous length of time even for a man floating in a life jacket. Research has shown the time limit for survival at that temperature (7°C) is a little over 3 hours. Full consciousness, and the ability to work to keep from drowning, is usually less than 2 hours. An unconscious victim is more likely to drown in splashing waves than to succumb to hypothermia.

So the searchers were as quick and efficient as they could be with the information they had. At 2:34 A.M., after Jonathan had been in the water about 3 hours, the rescue helicopter spotted him, and 13 minutes later they had him on board a lifeboat, but he could not be resuscitated. The coroner later ruled the cause of death as drowning. It was impossible to know whether he had taken in water in a reflexive gasp on entering the cold water or had drowned later after becoming unconscious. But as the subsequent investigation made clear, survival would have been more likely if he had used his tether or if electrical failure had not caused the engine and GPS problems.

Take It Easy

As soon as the sun set, and even before its glow faded and the coastal lights south of Cape Canaveral, Florida, showed, he realized how exhausted he was, and how long this night in March would be. He hadn't expected the wind to come up this much or to shift around this far to the north. The way he'd planned it weeks ago, he was simply going to sail a few miles farther offshore and ride the Gulf Stream north for a nice extra boost and a pleasant night's sail on a tropical breeze.

But the wind was too northerly and had raised furious standing waves in the Florida Current where it merged with the Gulf Stream. He'd sailed out not long after dawn just to see what the conditions were, but after clearing the Ft. Pierce Inlet into the Atlantic he almost immediately had found himself in 8-foot breaking seas that almost broached *Take It Easy*, his tired old 36-foot sloop, when he tried to escape back toward the coast with a quick tack. Yikes! It felt like it took him hours to reach calm water again, and he was worn out long before noon. Of course, being up half the night dealing with provisioning and last-minute boat issues hadn't helped.

Now it was dark again already, he hadn't even reached Cape Canaveral, and the wind and waves were still rising. Waves must be over 25, close to 30 feet now, he thought. He furled in a couple more wraps of the jib but was just too tired to get up and put a second reef in the main. Surely the wind would drop soon. At least it wasn't raining.

He pulled his iPhone out of his jeans pocket and thumbed open the chart app. There he was, a tiny red dot on the small screen, hovering an inch from the featureless coastline. He leaned against the wheel so he could steer with his elbows and keep both hands on the phone, the left holding it steady while he swiped and pinched with his right thumb and forefinger to move around on the screen and zoom in on what looked like Cape Canaveral somewhere ahead to the north. He looked up, hoping to see the lighthouse beacon in the distance, just as the bow fell off a wave and a sheet of spray soaked his face. Damn. He wiped the salt water from the face of the iPhone and stuck it back in his pocket.

More spray; the wind was still rising. The smart thing, he thought, would be to put in to shore, find a harbor, and get some rest. He didn't absolutely have to make it to St. Augustine by tomorrow night just because he'd planned it that way. A harbor would be nice. Just grab a beer and go to sleep.

Problem was he couldn't find what looked like a good harbor nearby. The long barrier islands were almost unbroken until he got farther north, and it would be sheer foolishness to anchor off the beach on a lee shore with this wind.

He took out his phone again and slid his finger around on the chart. Just below the tip of the cape was what looked like an inlet— or more probably a canal, since it seemed to be a straight line—that cut through the island to the broad Banana River inside. Along the canal were what looked like three dredged basins; maybe that was an anchorage? He zoomed in and tried to read the tiny type on the screen as he scrolled along the canal. "Restricted area" and "Security zone" labels were prominent, but he couldn't read the smaller type beneath them. The boat was moving too wildly in the waves, and he continually had to wipe spray from the screen. Near the entrance to the canal he saw a little sailboat symbol on the vector chart, finally got the crosshairs centered over it, and tapped for information. A marina! He tapped again. "Transient berths: No" appeared. And it looked like no room for anchoring.

Another burst of spray and he stuck the phone back in his pocket. He really should have brought a paper chart, he thought again, or at least a cruising guide. But he hadn't planned on stopping before St. Augustine, and he'd sailed all last summer with just the phone chart app, so how was he to know he'd need a paper chart? The old ones were getting mildewed anyway, so he'd left them at home.

The other thing about entering an unfamiliar inlet at night was that he didn't know if he'd pass a Coast Guard station or a local harbormaster in there, and there was that problem with the running lights. He'd been sure that he would have time during the day to find the broken circuit or blown fuse and get them working before dark, but the autopilot wasn't working either so he'd been stuck hand-steering all day. He didn't know for sure but thought there might be a pretty hefty fine for no running lights. And then they might start looking for other things, like charts, fire extinguishers, and all that stuff he planned to install on the boat once he restored or replaced the big things. The trouble with boats, he thought, was that you never get caught up.

Man, was he exhausted. The wind seemed to have shifted even farther north and was driving him a little west of north, toward land, regardless of how much he pinched it. In the distance ahead, just starboard of the bow, he saw a tiny light. Damn. Now he'd have to tack east again to clear the cape. Had he worked in that close to the coast already? Was he already west of the cape's longitude?

He should have bought that new compass for the boat. The phone's compass was terrible for navigation.

He thought about tacking. He thought about putting a second reef in first, but it was blowing pretty hard now and he was heeled over about 30 degrees close-hauled, and it would be impossible to do the reef without help from the autopilot. He might start the engine and motor straight into the wind long enough to reef, but he wasn't sure if the engine would start and he just didn't want to deal with that right now. Tomorrow it would be easier in the sunlight and with lighter wind. He could go offshore a bit, ride the Gulf Stream up as he'd planned, get the boat fixed up, and grab some catnaps along the way.

Meanwhile, the wind continued to drive him toward a lee shore. He was so tired. He just wanted a 5-minute nap, but he wasn't dumb enough to close his eyes on this course.

So he got ready to tack. He wrapped the starboard lazy jib-sheet around its winch and moved the winch handle to the pocket on that side. With his feet braced and his right hand clutching the wheel, he carefully uncleated the port sheet and shook out its tangles so it would run free. He peered forward into the dark and caught another sheet of spray in the face. Damn, just do it.

He spun the wheel to starboard and the boat began turning immediately. It was head to wind faster than he'd anticipated, however, and he was too slow to release the port sheet. The jib backed, the bow blew across rapidly with the help of the waves now slamming its port side, and the sheet jammed. In a flash the boat was broadside to the wind, and with the jib backwinded and the mainsheet still tight, he lost all steering. The boat heeled far over to starboard, and he lost his footing and tumbled to the rail. The water was almost at the level of the cockpit coaming. He reached back, his fingers found the binnacle guard, and he pulled himself upright. For a terrible long moment he thought the boat was going over, a complete knockdown, but it steadied long enough for him to claw up to the high port winch and free the jibsheet. With a roar the sail blew across and cracked in the wind like a demon. But the boat stayed pinned over until he reached the mainsheet, which was under terrific tension now, and finally managed to release it also.

The boat came up to a heel of only 20 degrees and, his arms and legs shaking, his muscles limp, he collapsed on the lower cockpit seat and covered his head and ears with his hands to block the furor of flapping sails and flailing lines.

For a long minute he just sat and waited for something more to happen, feeling certain some final awful thing was about to occur. He had almost capsized during a simple tack. Now the mast would likely come down or the hull would split open beneath him.

But all that happened was the furious noise of the sails flogging. Eventually he moved slowly to the mainsheet, got it wrapped on the winch drum, and found a winch handle. He started cranking it in just to ease the ruckus, not even sure where the bow was pointed or how the rudder was set.

It took what felt like an hour before he'd regained control and had *Take It Easy* sailing again. Judging from the coast lights at his back and the wind on the port beam, he was apparently sailing southeast. Maybe toward Bimini. Definitely toward the Gulf Stream, which wasn't all that many miles away.

The wind had not dropped, though.

He would have to go back hard on the wind again to continue north.

He leaned against the wheel and closed his eyes for a moment. Then he reached into his pocket for his phone. It wouldn't come on. He knew the battery wasn't that low yet. He felt the wet fabric of his jeans and realized the phone had gotten soaked in salt water.

In the dark he couldn't read his watch to see how long it was until dawn. Somewhere down below he had a flashlight, which he hadn't thought to keep in the cockpit because he always had his phone, with its nifty flashlight app, on him.

He didn't dare lock the wheel and go below. With these waves the boat would almost immediately jibe or tack if left unattended and the whole nightmare would start all over again.

He looked around the cockpit, trying to imagine another 6 to 7 hours of this in the dark. He took a moment to coil the sheet ends and straighten up the cockpit. He sat on the high side, one hand on the wheel, and watched the waves. Then he looked back around the boat, eyes coming to rest on the new handheld VHF clipped to the binnacle, a recent Christmas gift from his parents. He looked at it a long time. It hadn't been on today, so the charge should be good. It was a submersible type, so the spray shouldn't have affected it. And it was brand new, so it shouldn't have broken yet.

He didn't think he was supposed to make a Mayday call if he wasn't actually sinking or something. He waited a minute to think about what to say if he was lucky enough to be heard. But he couldn't think; he was too exhausted.

In the end he simply turned it on, confirmed the channel on 16, thumbed the mic, and said, "Coast Guard? This is the sailboat *Take It Easy*."

•••— — —•••

It took the Coast Guard cutter only an hour to reach him. Two crew boarded and helped him get the sails down, and then they got him aboard the cutter and took the sailboat in tow. He had some difficulty trying to explain how he'd gotten into this situation without sounding foolish, but the crew were nice enough to say that being too exhausted to continue safely was cause enough for their assistance. Back in port, they filed their report, and the next day the sector issued a routine press release about another successful search-and-rescue case, ending with the usual phrasing that even though there had been no injuries, the case could have easily turned fatal, followed by a list of required and recommended safety gear all mariners should carry.

Briefly

Ottawa River, Ottawa, Canada, August 2011. It was just a simple excursion on the Ottawa River, sailing a ways downstream, then motoring back against the current if the wind grew light, upstream toward the park, and then doing it again. It was a fine early evening, and the three people on the daysailer were enjoying the last hours of daylight. Then, without warning, the outboard motor stalled and they started drifting downstream. One person kept pulling the starter rope and fiddling with the choke and throttle, the second trimmed the sails and tried to keep the boat moving against the current, and the third looked downstream to where ripples on the water indicated the increasing current as the river approached the rapids. "We better call for help!" he said. He called 911 on his cell and was transferred to the fire department, which operated the water-rescue team. The sailors were advised to drop their anchor before the boat reached the rapids, which they hadn't thought of, and that stopped them long enough for the rescue boat to reach them. Funny what you don't think of in a crisis.

Galveston Bay, Texas, 2007. The couple had a few drinks and then decided to go for a short sail. Conditions seemed good, with only a light chop on the water and a good wind for sailing. They climbed into the small daysailer at the dock, started the outboard, and motored out into the bay. They'd gone only a hundred yards when a gust of wind blew off the man's hat. He reached for it, lost his balance, and tumbled over into the water. He was a good swimmer, his wife said later, and she expected him to swim right back to the boat. She took the motor out of gear and waited for him. But the wind was blowing the boat away from him. She didn't think to throw him a life jacket. When she put the outboard back in gear, the engine stalled and it took her a long time to get it started, she said later, explaining why it had taken her so long to get back to shore to call for help. His body was found later.

Lake Michigan, Wisconsin, August 2011. Sometimes it just seems like nothing goes right. The morning had started just fine, a bit breezy but good, as the 61-year-old sailed his 32-footer solo out into the lake. When the wind built too strong for comfort, he decided to turn into a harbor for shelter, but as he started to furl the jib the furling line jammed on the drum. He couldn't get it free while still trying to sail, so he sailed on down the lakeshore a short distance to the next, larger harbor where he was able to turn in. He started the inboard engine, planning to motor slowly up into the wind with the wheel locked while he went forward to free the jammed furler, but when he put the engine in gear, it died immediately. He looked back and saw his towed dinghy blown up against the transom, its painter disappearing down into the water. It had probably wrapped on the prop shaft. So now his only option was to sail around until conditions improved. But when he looked down the companionway he saw water over the floorboards; could the pressure on the shaft have loosened the shaft-log seal? He couldn't go forward to fix the sail, and he couldn't go below to check the leak. While he pondered his dilemma a wind shift caught the boat sideways and pushed it up against the breakwater at the harbor entrance, and he heard the nasty grinding of fiberglass against rock. He reached for the VHF and called the Coast Guard. Luckily they had a 41-foot cutter inside the harbor and were there within minutes, taking him in tow and bringing aboard a fast pump if needed for the leak. Less than an hour later, he'd regained his composure and was telling jokes as the marina hoisted his dripping boat from the water.

CHAPTER 7

A Gust of Wind

*S**mall sailboats—like catamarans, Sunfish, and unballasted day-sailers—are known to capsize easily and often in wind gusts or if the sailor loses control of the sails or does not maintain a good balance of crew weight. For the sailors of such boats it is especially important to wear a PFD as well as to be prepared to right the boat or, failing that, to stay with the boat and call for help. As these incidents show, a simple capsize can otherwise quickly become a disaster.*

Three Generations Sailing off Puffin Island

The July day dawned bright and beautiful, a perfect day for sailing from North Wales to Puffin Island and beyond in the family's new sailing dinghy. And what a day they had planned! Mr. Roberts, in his mid-sixties, was looking forward to a great day on the water with his son, who was in his late thirties, whom he still called Junior, and his two young grandsons, Tommy, age 8, and Hayden, age 11. The boys had not sailed before, but Roberts and Junior had sailed the new dinghy six or seven times already and were confident the boys would have a great time. At 4 meters overall, the boat was a bit cramped for the four of them. Its capacity plate limited it to three passengers, but they figured the two boys added up to only the weight of one man. Besides, it was beamy enough to feel quite stable.

Roberts and Junior had talked about the day and were not concerned about taking the small craft a short ways offshore. They had already sailed it along the coast of North Wales without incident. They even discussed what they'd do if it capsized and how to right it. It had plenty of buoyancy as long as the hatches of the cuddy cabin were secured, and the centerboard provided enough leverage to flip it back upright if it was blown over. The morning weather forecast on television was good, with no severe weather or high winds mentioned.

And they took their usual safety precautions. All four wore PFDs. Roberts never drank, since he was on medication for an irregular heartbeat, and Junior had nothing to drink before or while sailing.

For more than 30 years Roberts had cruised the Welsh coast in his motor cabin cruiser, but in his sixties he became interested in sailing as a more relaxing family pastime. When he saw the new dinghy at a boat show 4 months ago, he'd fallen in love with its lines and the idea of sailing with his son and grandsons, and had bought it on the spot.

They launched the boat off the trailer late in the morning at a boat ramp in Conwy Bay. In a light wind they started the small outboard engine, raised the mainsail, and headed out into the bay.

Soon enough, the wind built and they shut off the outboard and continued under mainsail alone. It was fine sailing, and the boys were excited as the water swirled by the hull. Their destination was Red Wharf Bay, a few nautical miles to the northwest, past Puffin Island. The wind was southwest, giving them a nice beam reach on port tack. There was just enough room in the cockpit for all four of them to sit in a row on the port cockpit seat.

Junior was aft, steering with the tiller and holding the mainsheet in his other hand. Occasionally the wind gusted, but he kept the dinghy on an even keel by letting out the sail whenever they heeled very much. Next to him, Roberts relaxed, feeling proud of how well his son was handling the boat. Forward of Roberts the two young boys simply held on and enjoyed the ride.

For 2 hours they sailed without having to tack or do much at all as Puffin Island grew larger on the horizon.

"Great sail, eh, boys?" Roberts would say, and they would grin.

By two o'clock the wind was getting stronger as they approached the island, still blowing in from the southwest, and Roberts realized the ride would likely get wet soon after they rounded the island and made a close-hauled course to the west for Red Wharf Bay. They were all dressed only in shorts and T-shirts, plus he was wearing a windbreaker, but the sun was warm. With the growing wind, however, the sea had become choppy, with waves rising to 1.5 meters, and soon they were being splashed by spray over the bow. The water was 26°C and felt cold on their sun-warmed skin. Soon Tommy said he was cold. They let him crawl into the cuddy and put the dropboards back in place to keep it dry.

As the wind increased still more, maybe up to 25 knots now, Junior was having trouble holding the mainsheet in one hand while he steered. He took a turn of the line around the cleat beside him to take up the strain but kept a grip on the line so he could let it out quickly if needed.

At 2:30 Junior's wife called on his mobile phone. "Great sailing!" he shouted over the wind. "We're just off Puffin Island now. If the breeze keeps up we'll reach Red Wharf in about an hour."

She wanted to talk more and hear what their sons thought of the sailing, but he said he needed both hands to control the boat so they rang off.

It may have been that the island funneled more wind on them, or maybe a wind storm was brewing, for a strong gust hit them just as he got his phone back in his pocket. The boat abruptly headed up, turning to port while Junior pulled hard on the tiller to straighten it out. But it was too late; water poured over the port coaming into the cockpit, and with all their weight on that side the dinghy rolled to port and went over.

Then the three of them were in the cold water, joined quickly by Tommy, who threw out the dropboards and pulled himself out of the cuddy as the boat rolled. With the push of the waves the boat continued rolling and turned turtle, water splashing over the inverted hull.

Junior checked that everyone was floating and seemed okay, and then shivering with cold climbed up onto the hull to reach the centerboard, which had swung partway back into its trunk. He extended the board, grasped its end, and pulled back with his body weight.

The boat rolled, slowly at first but quickly gathering speed with the increasing leverage of the board, but then kept rolling over the top of Junior.

He splashed back up to try it again, this time easing his pressure on the centerboard as the boat came upright. This time it stayed upright. The cockpit was full of water, the cabin dropboards were missing, and the cabin was at least partly flooded. He checked that the mainsheet was not cleated down so hopefully they could avoid getting knocked down by the wind again.

But it only took a few seconds for the waves to push the boat over again, and once more it turned turtle.

Junior turned from the boat to his family in the water. The boys were flailing about in their flotation aids, their teeth chattering and their faces white, but they seemed okay for the moment. His father, however, seemed barely able to tread water. He realized then that his flotation device hadn't inflated. Quickly Junior swam to him and towed him back to the hull, where he felt around in the water and finally pulled the toggle line to inflate the PFD. His father's face looked bloodless.

On the other side of the hull, Tommy was gasping and coughing up water, having trouble in the waves. Junior quickly got to him and managed to push him up onto the hull, but Tommy seemed unable to hang on to the centerboard and slipped back into the cold water. Junior got him up again, then hoisted up Hayden. Again Tommy was slipping off, shaking with cold, and Junior had to keep pushing up against Tommy's legs and feet. Hayden was able to stay on the hull on his own, but Junior didn't dare release Tommy. After a minute he called to his father but didn't hear an answer. He started moving back around the boat to check on him, but Tommy started sliding down again so he stayed where he was to hold him up.

It was a terrible decision, having to stay with his son and hope his father could make it on his own. Hayden was not strong enough to hold on himself and support Tommy on the hull. Now Tommy wasn't moving; was he unconscious?

The waves were slapping his own face and he was coughing up water. He didn't know what to do. It took all his energy to hold up his son and try to keep his own mouth free of water.

After a little while he heard the engine of a boat some distance away, but he had no way to signal it. Their flares were in the cabin underwater, and he didn't dare try to swim down to look for them. With his last bit of strength he hauled himself higher on the hull and waved frantically at the passing boat.

They didn't see him.

From his higher position, before sliding back down the hull, Junior saw Roberts floating a short distance away from the hull, not moving. The inflated PFD had ridden up his torso and shoulders, and his face was near the water being splashed by waves.

But he couldn't leave his sons. Tommy was unconscious, and he couldn't tell whether he was breathing. He was a whitish-blue color all over.

Junior finally thought to fish his mobile phone from his wet shorts, but it was dead.

His mind raced and then strangely went blank.

Almost an hour later another boat passed. He was so cold he barely noticed it at first, but then he roused himself and waved. The fishing boat turned and approached. Even before the boat reached them its skipper was calling for help on his VHF radio. Junior looked around, but his father had drifted out of sight.

The fishing boat came alongside, and with the help of its crew they got Tommy aboard. One of the men started CPR. Junior and Hayden were taken aboard and wrapped in blankets.

The skipper radioed the Coastguard again for urgent medical attention for Tommy and reported that a man was still missing in the water. A helicopter was launched, and a water search began with lifeboats.

It did not take long for the helicopter to reach them, and Tommy was winched aboard and flown to the nearest hospital.

Roberts's body was found facedown in the water about a half mile away.

The helicopter returned shortly and evacuated Hayden to the hospital.

Tommy was pronounced dead on arrival at the hospital. Roberts's body was taken to shore in the lifeboat. The postmortems later ruled that Roberts died from a combination of drowning and hypothermia and Tommy died of hypothermia.

Junior and Hayden recovered.

••• – – – •••

The UK Marine Accident Investigation Branch (MAIB) conducted a thorough investigation of the incident. Among its conclusions were the following. The foreign-built sailboat did not meet UK stability and buoyancy requirements and could not be easily righted after capsize, although the owner could not have known this. The crew had insufficient dinghy-sailing experience for the conditions they experienced, and they wore clothing providing little protection against the cold. They had not received the latest marine forecast of deteriorating weather. Roberts's PFD was not securely fastened with a tight waist belt. They had no accessible means to signal or call for help.

A Hobie on the Lake

Lake Hefner is a large recreational lake in the northwest section of Oklahoma City. Flanked by a golf course on one side and circled by a bike path, it is an easily accessed urban oasis popular for picnicking, fishing, and other water recreation. Since personal watercraft, waterskiing, and fast motorboats are banned, it is particularly popular for sailing, and sports a wide variety of sailboats seldom seen so far from America's coasts. With a marina and active boat club, even larger cabin boats call the 2,500-acre lake home. The land surrounding the lake is flat, allowing steady, often exciting breezes.

There are sail races almost every summer weekend, and kiteboarding too has become popular. Casual sailors can rent Hobie catamarans, and others trailer their boats here or launch small daysailers from the beach.

It is a family-friendly lake, ringed by parks, playgrounds, and places to eat. On weekends it seems kids are everywhere, on land and water. Sometimes the water feels like a large playground itself, there are so many boats out. But that gives the lake a welcoming, safe feeling. Who could find anything to worry about when you're surrounded by so many others?

That was the atmosphere the Saturday that Mike and his friend Jerry planned to take Mike's two kids sailing in his new Hobie 16. With the help of a couple teenagers they launched the cat, and Mike's kids, Christine, 8, and Josh, 6, ran off for an ice cream while Mike and Jerry stepped the mast, rigged the boat, and bent on the sails.

"Get your life jackets," Mike told the kids when they came back. "Leave everything else in the car, and we'll have a picnic after we sail for a while."

Mike and Jerry stood in the shallows holding the Hobie steady while the kids climbed aboard. Josh looked almost lost inside his life jacket, as Mike had bought them large enough to last a couple years as the kids grew. His own life jacket, like Jerry's, was old and a little frayed. He'd grown up nearby and had gotten a lot of use from it over the years.

What a day! The wind felt like a steady 12 to 15 knots from the southwest, great for sailing a Hobie Cat. Out on the lake, off the aptly named Hobie Point, he could see half a dozen boats already zipping along; the more experienced sailors were flying hull as they beat into the wind. The kids were going to love this! With this many boats sailing and surely more to come, there would probably be some impromptu racing too. That excited Jerry, a Laser sailor who didn't know much about Hobies but was eager to learn.

Mike pointed to where he wanted Christine and Josh to sit, one on each side of the trapeze, forward and out of the way. "Hang on, kids!" he said with a grin, and he and Jerry pushed the Hobie deeper, dropped the rudders, and climbed aboard.

They pointed out at the middle of the lake, the breeze across the starboard beam, and took off. As they accelerated rapidly, Mike motioned for Jerry to slide over and join him on the starboard edge of the trapeze. "Let's stay flat for a while," he said, "no use scaring the kids until they get used to it."

He looked over at his kids. Christine was grinning, strands of hair coming loose from her ponytail and flying around her face. Josh looked more somber, his knuckles white from his grip on the trapeze frame.

On a little gust Mike felt the starboard hull start to rise, and he immediately turned more to port to flatten the boat. "Spill some wind," he told Jerry, who was controlling the mainsheet, "at least until we see what the wind's doing."

Within minutes they were several hundred yards off the beach, closing on another boat ahead.

"Having fun, guys?" he shouted at the kids.

"Yeah!" Christine yelled back, and Josh nodded.

Experienced sailors righting a Hobie catamaran. (Henrik Dalgaard)

Then it was time to tack. Mike explained to the kids what they were about to do, again emphasizing that their main job was just to hang on. "Once you get used to it," he promised, "I'll let both of you help steer."

When everyone was ready, he shouted, "Helm's alee!" and he and Jerry ducked and scrambled under the boom as he turned to starboard.

It wasn't the most graceful tack, Mike thought as he headed up on port tack, moving toward the lake's western shore. But they hadn't lost all their speed and had jumped on the new course quick enough. He looked back over his shoulder at the other Hobies and noticed that one with red sails had gone over. As he watched, the two sailors in the water flipped it back upright and climbed aboard.

"Let's do it again," he said. "Ready to tack?"

Maybe he should have waited until he heard Jerry say "Ready," or maybe Jerry had just gotten hung up with the sheets or wasn't paying attention. In any case, when he turned sharply and slid across to starboard, Jerry didn't follow him. Mike's steering was perfect; within a couple seconds the sails filled and shot the boat forward as the starboard hull rose and he felt the reduced control as the starboard rudder came out of the water. Then, before he could correct the helm or shout at Jerry to release the sheet, a gust knocked the boat over.

Mike catapulted into the water clear of the boat. Because of the flotation bulb at the top of the mast, the boat floated mostly on its side and canted only slightly past vertical with the starboard hull in the air above him. Christine floated in the water a few feet from the port hull, apparently okay, but Josh had managed to hang on to the starboard rail and was dangling with his feet a couple feet above the water. He looked terrified.

"Josh! It's okay to let go!" Mike shouted as he breast-stroked back to the boat, his motion hampered by his life jacket, which rose high on his shoulders. "Just let go, buddy! I got you!"

Jerry was at the aft end of the port hull by the rudder, keeping out of the way.

Josh let go and splashed into the water just as Mike reached him. In a moment he was bobbing alongside Christine, his small face grim between the wings of his life jacket, which was floating high up on his body. "Okay, buddy?" Josh nodded. "See, it's not so bad. I guess I should've told you that could happen, but I didn't want to scare you."

Christine had managed to paddle over, fighting her life jacket, and put one hand on Josh's shoulder, holding his life-jacket strap. "What do we do now, Dad?" she said, trying to sound cheerful.

"Now we get the boat back up!" he said. "I want you two guys to stay together on this side. Don't come close to the boat, and keep away from the mast. Jerry and I are going around to the other side, and we'll climb up and pull the other hull backward into the water. You guys just watch, okay? Just stay together, and I'll come back and get you when the boat's ready."

"Okay, Dad," they said in unison.

Mike and Jerry worked their way around the hull to the other side. Jerry looked up at the hull, which seemed an impossible height above them. "This is easy in a Laser," he said. "You just stand on the centerboard and lean back. But I'm clueless what to do with a cat."

Mike studied the hulls and the frame and bottom of the trapeze. "It's the same principle. We just climb up there and grab the hull and lean back to lever it over."

"Climb where?"

"Well, I haven't actually done it before. But how hard can it be?"

For the next 5 minutes, they struggled to right the catamaran. It was tiring work. The float at the top of the mast kept the cat from turning turtle, but it was difficult to climb up on the lower hull and then stand to reach the high hull. Their feet kept slipping, and Mike's arms were getting tired from pulling himself up repeatedly.

He noticed the kids had drifted farther away from the other side of the boat and realized that he and Jerry needed to move more quickly.

"My life jacket's slowing me down," he called to Jerry. "I can climb up better without it getting in the way."

They both removed their life jackets and looped the buckles around the trapeze frame.

"Dad!" called Christine. "I can't pull Josh back to the boat!"

He looked again and saw they had drifted another 10 feet farther away. "Just a minute!" he called. "We'll come get you in just a minute!"

They climbed up again and grasped the upper hull to pull it back, but as he leaned all his weight back, Mike's hands slipped and he fell back in the water. He felt beat. "Let's go get the kids," he called to Jerry.

They pulled themselves around the lower hull and began swimming to the children. Jerry, the stronger swimmer, took the lead and reached them first. Christine was having trouble holding on to Josh, who was lower in the water as his loose life jacket rose above his thin shoulders. Jerry told Christine to try to tighten her own life-jacket's buckles as he worked on Josh's. When Mike finally joined them, he treaded water while Josh held on to his neck and shoulders as Jerry struggled to tighten the straps. He looked over once at Mike, whose face had gone blank as he moved his arms and legs slowly in the water.

"Okay," Jerry said at last. "C'mon, Christine, you hold on to Josh while I tow you two back to the boat. Make a chain." He watched as Josh released his hold on Mike. "Mike," he called, "follow us. Let's go!"

With Josh's arms tight around his neck, Jerry started a slow breaststroke back toward the Hobie. It was slow going towing both kids.

When he was 20 feet from the lower hull, he paused and treaded water a moment, looking back. He couldn't see Mike; he simply wasn't there. He pulled Josh's hands from his neck and kicked hard in the water trying to rise higher to look over the waves for bubbles or any sign of Mike beneath the surface but saw nothing. Now Josh was panicking, crying and slipping down in his life jacket again, his mouth too near the water. Christine was frantically turning in the water looking for her father.

He had to secure the kids first, he knew that. He grabbed Josh's arms and wrapped them back around his neck, told Christine to hold on, and kicked for the boat, fighting the impulse to keep looking back. Finally they reached the hull. He helped Christine get one arm around the trapeze frame, got her other one to grip Josh's shoulders, and swam back to where he thought Mike must have gone under.

He dived beneath the murky brown water and stroked, rose for air, dived and stroked again, and again. Every so often he checked that the kids were still holding on. He kept at it, diving and swimming underwater, unable to see more than a foot or so through the murk, trying for expanding circles in his search, until he was so tired he could barely stay afloat himself when he surfaced. Finally he had to return to the boat and rest. It took a long time for him to get back to the boat, and his muscles were rigid and quivering when he reached it.

A fishing boat finally came alongside and then radioed for help.

Divers found Mike's body the next morning. The coroner later ruled that he had drowned but could not explain why he had gone under so quickly.

Briefly

Connecticut, 2008. An 18-year-old sailing instructor was teaching three young children to sail on a 17-foot catamaran. There was no chase boat. When a gust capsized the cat, all four ended up in the water. The instructor was able to reach and hold on to two of the children, but the youngest, wearing a Type III PFD, drifted away from the capsized sailboat. By the time the instructor got to the young child, about 10 minutes after the capsize, he had drowned.

New South Wales, Australia, 2011. Five people were aboard the 17-foot Shark Cat catamaran when it capsized not far from shore in the early afternoon. The incident was observed by a nearby jet-skier, who managed to save one woman. A couple in their seventies and a 12-year-old girl were pulled from the water shortly afterward but could not be revived. Emergency officials searched for a fourth victim, a 47-year-old man not wearing a life jacket, but eventually had to call off the search after being unable to locate his body.

Rehoboth Bay, Delaware, August 2011. A 63-year-old man and his friend were sailing in a small daysailer about half a mile offshore when it capsized in a gust. Neither was wearing a life jacket. The crew was able to stay with the capsized boat, but the older man could not hold on and drifted away. He was unconscious by the time emergency responders arrived and was pronounced dead shortly after. There was no sign that he had been injured in the capsize.

Massachusetts, October 2009. A father, an experienced sailor, and his son were sailing their Sunfish near shore when they lost control of the boat in a gust of wind. The boat capsized, throwing them both into the water. Neither wore a PFD. The son swam over to the Sunfish, which was drifting away, and tried to right the boat. He was close enough to shore that he was able to ground the boat but lost sight of his father. He called to his brother on shore to call 911 for help. Shortly thereafter the harbormaster recovered the unresponsive man and began CPR, but he could not be resuscitated.

CHAPTER 8

No Way to Call for Help

*A*s we have seen in previous chapters, many boating emergencies develop quickly. A crisis can become life threatening in seconds or minutes, especially when someone is in the water. Other emergencies may begin with an unexpected but not immediately dangerous incident and then gradually become more serious over time, such as when a boat capsizes or a sailor is separated from the boat but is able to stay afloat with the help of a PFD or by hanging on to the capsized boat. In these cases, nevertheless, the situation can become life threatening if the boat cannot be righted or the sailor cannot be recovered back onto the boat or if rescue does not occur in time. Many sailors and other boaters fail to consider this possibility and do not carry a means to call for help. In that misfortunate situation, survival may depend on whether another boat happens by or another chance event.*

Voices

She heard voices around her in the water, so she knew she was still alive. Wouldn't it mean that? But she was so tired she could no longer open her eyes. Her mind kept drifting, floating, much as she was floating in the water. Was she still floating? Was she still in the water? There were splashes, she heard those too. She no longer felt cold. In fact, she couldn't feel her body at all, as if it had floated away, except when something moved, like James's arm around her shoulders. Yes. He was still there beside her.

James. His strong arm. He must be holding her up, she thought, but then she couldn't feel him either. His voice was so soft she wasn't sure it was really there. "Hold on," he said, a murmur in her ear. Was it really him? "You have to hold on."

Voices.

"Is she still alive?" That was the boy. Farther off, the girl was crying, or maybe that was the waves. Were they still on the boat?

"I'll hold her up, Dad. You need to take a break."

"You have to hold on."

"Why doesn't anyone come?" The girl, hysterical.

But the sun was so warm. In the lazy heat of the afternoon the scent of flowers was overwhelming. No wind, and the dragonflies were flitting everywhere. The lake shimmered below the lawn, catching the light, and somewhere far off she heard the sounds of children laughing. How happy she was that James had brought her to this wonderful place! James and his silly boat; it took a windless day to keep him on land. They walked the shore arm in arm, like old married couples do. Not so old, she almost giggled.

How old? What an odd thing to think, and for a moment she realized she wasn't fully in charge of her thinking.

He skipped stones over the flat water. Four, five, six skips.

"Just hold on a little longer."

Something bit her ear, an angry bee from the flowers—no, it was cold. A wave? In the garden? That seemed long ago, as if there were still time.

"Why hasn't anyone seen us yet? Why isn't anyone coming?" She heard panic in the girl's voice, almost as if—as if someone was dying.

Maybe she was just hungry. They hadn't eaten yet. It was too bouncy to open the picnic basket; things would fly off every which way! Someone would spill the wine!

"It's the cold."

"No, the water's not that cold. Not yet."

"It is."

James's strong arm around her. Dancing—if only she'd known him when they were young. Dear James. How wonderful it felt to sleep in his arms.

"Try your phone again—please, just try it!"

"It's not going to work. It's dead."

There, someone had said it. But it wasn't her, she must still be alive, she heard their voices.

"It wasn't your fault, Dad," Was that his son, Carter? He spoke so seldom, she wasn't sure he liked her. Or maybe he didn't approve of her; it had been only a few years since his mother had died.

Those were not her thoughts. No. Carter brought them sandwiches in the garden. He shooed away the bees attracted to the wine.

"Please, Dad, let me help!"

No warmth, and she missed even the cold. Why was that? All these people in the bedroom, all that talking keeping her awake.

"Look, I see someone on shore! Why don't they see us?"

James murmuring. Soothing. "Try to pull yourself up higher. Try to wave." Who were they waving at? The neighbors across the garden?

So tired. Perhaps she'd take a nap before getting ready for dinner. Then they were going dancing again.

"I have you," he murmured. "Just hold on a little longer."

She felt his strong arms. They lifted her, gently swaying, and she surrendered into them.

$$\bullet\bullet\bullet - - - \bullet\bullet\bullet$$

These sailors were heading back across Lake St. Clair, returning home to Michigan after a few days' vacation in Belle River, Ontario. On board were James, an experienced sailor not quite 60, his companion, Irene, 63, his son, Carter, and the two children of a friend, all of them wearing life jackets. It should have been just a pleasant day sail only half a mile offshore on a 23-foot sailboat that had withstood much stronger conditions. The wind was getting up but was not too bad, but then the water humped up over the shoals and a 6-foot wave caught them out of the blue and flipped the boat. They had no way to call for help, and no other boats were nearby. They were in the water for an hour and a half, clinging to the overturned hull, before finally they were seen and a good Samaritan on a boat rushed the woman, unconscious but still breathing, to paramedics waiting on shore. Sadly, 2 hours later she died in the hospital without regaining consciousness.

Short Sail on the Sound

Albemarle Sound on the coast of North Carolina is typically full of boats on a summer afternoon, and sailors in most areas seldom feel isolated. But when a thunderstorm threatens, most boats seek shelter and those caught on the water can find themselves terribly alone.

Paul and Karen planned to sail their 14-foot Sunfish for only an hour or so to cool off on this hot July afternoon. The earlier forecast had included a chance of afternoon popup thunderstorms, but the sky was clear and the wind moderate so they weren't worried. Besides, it would only be a short sail within a mile of the south shore, so it should take only 20 minutes or so to get back if they saw a storm building.

At 3:30 P.M. they launched the Sunfish and took off out into the sound. The wind was hot and from the west and light as usual close to shore. But a west wind meant an easy beam reach north out into open water where hopefully the air would be cooler and the wind fresher. Still, with the late-July water temperature in the low 80s, they couldn't hope for much of a cooling breeze.

They wore only swimsuits. It was too hot and sticky for life jackets, which they stowed in the aft cubby space in the boat's small cockpit.

The Sunfish eased along at only a couple knots, Karen trailing one hand in the water and occasionally splashing herself in an effort to cool off. Paul kept dipping his cap in the water and pouring it over his head. Just another hot Carolina summer day.

After half an hour of easy sailing they tacked the boat around to head back home. In the distance to the south the sky was the funny brown color of a dust storm. The wind had all but died, and as they bobbed in the small waves they watched the southern sky grow darker. Abruptly the wind came back but was now from the south—the direction they needed to go. Paul turned east to tack back toward home. Karen moved over to the starboard side to add her weight to his to counteract the heeling as Paul tried to turn more to the south. But the south wind was still building and he worried they'd be blown over, so he let out the sheet and spilled some wind. They were making no progress to the south at all. If anything, they were being blown north as they sailed east, farther out into the sound.

They were startled by how quickly the waves were building from the south, making it even more difficult to turn toward shore. To keep the boat flat and under control, Paul had gradually fallen farther off the wind and was now on a broad reach northeast.

Shortly after the first hard gust shook them, Karen heard a rumble of thunder from the south. This wasn't just a wind or dust storm, they suddenly realized.

"I really don't want to be out here in lightning," she said in a low tone. She looked around and couldn't find another boat anywhere in sight.

Paul was studying the shoreline in three directions. The sound continued on to the east—nowhere to go that way. The south shore was nearest but impossible to get to. The marshes to the west were closer than the north shore, but to go west they'd have to tack or jibe, and the wind was strong enough now to make either a risk.

"We have to go across the sound," he said. "It's farther but easier to sail, and maybe we can stay ahead of the storm." He tried to sound optimistic but could practically hear her doing the math in her head. It was maybe 5 or 6 miles across the sound to the safety of the bay near Edenton, which would take almost an hour.

The thunder grew louder and the wind gustier as they sailed on a fast plane north. The wind had shifted slightly to the west at least, giving Paul hope they could make it into the bay without having to tack.

Then another gust hit just as the starboard side was slapped by a large wave, and the Sunfish was knocked over. In the water beside it, they watched as the wind and waves turned the boat all the way over, inverting the hull.

The first thing he noticed, once he was sure that Karen was okay, was that the daggerboard was not jutting out of its slot in the hull as it should have been. Something must have broken, or perhaps the force of capsizing had somehow slammed it out the other side. He could only hope it was still held to the boat by the bungee cord. Then he might be able to go underwater and insert it to provide the leverage to right the boat.

Karen was not thinking about the daggerboard but was watching the sky overhead, and worrying about lightning. Angry clouds swirled overhead and rain was just beginning. What happened if lightning struck the water near you? She knew water conducted electricity—a terrifying thought.

Her fingers were already sore from gripping the boat's slick hull. The waves were making it harder to keep her face out of the water.

"You think the life jackets are still in the boat?" she shouted at Paul.

Paul looked at her, then dived under. After about 20 seconds he emerged with both life jackets.

They got them on and were hanging on to the hull a minute later when the thunderstorm struck. Hard rain pelted their heads and shoulders and stung their eyes with the wind. The waves slamming the little Sunfish around made it hard to hold on.

They hoped the storm would blow by as quickly as it had come, but no such luck. Paul looked frequently at his waterproof watch. After an hour they were still in the thick of it, the air full of water, blotting out the dark clouds overhead. Lightning was all around them, and they wearied of counting seconds between flashes and the following booms to see how close the strikes were. Once there was a deafening crack almost simultaneous with the flash and Karen steeled herself, expecting a shock, but nothing happened. The storm just kept raging, the waves growing higher. After the first hour they stopped talking and kept their mouths closed against the chaotic splashing against and over the hull. Each kept their own thoughts; Karen was frightened by the lightning and wondered how long it would be before they could get back to shore when the storm passed, and Paul was vowing that next time he'd check the radar with his weather app before setting out. He also thought about buying a dry bag to bring along a cell phone.

Finally, after some 2 hours, the rain and wind slowly diminished, and eventually the rain stopped. But the boat was still being tossed about by the waves. It took another hour for the water to calm enough for them to try to climb up onto the inverted hull that offered no handholds. Even though the water temperature was in the low 80s, they were chilled after being in the water for 3 hours, But they warmed up a little as their skin dried.

By now it was dusk and they could see lights coming on along the shore. Paul guessed they were 3 or 4 miles from the nearest shore.

"Can we get the boat upright now?" Karen asked.

Paul shook his head. "I felt around in the water when I went under for the life jackets. The daggerboard's gone."

She stared at him; she hadn't expected this. "So we can't get back? There's nothing at all we can do?"

He shook his head again and mumbled, "Sorry."

They sat in silence as it grew darker, and eventually the stars began coming out. After about an hour they heard the distant sound of a boat engine and at last spotted its running lights at least a mile away, but it wasn't coming in their direction.

"Maybe someone will see us," she said.

Paul was thinking he should also get a strobe light to keep in the dry bag he was going to buy. And they should have told someone they were going sailing, someone who would have noticed when they were late getting back.

Another hour passed. They watched planes flying far overhead and looked for more boats, maybe someone coming back late from a fishing trip—but who would have been that foolish to stay out in such a storm?

They had given up hope of rescue and were thinking about how they'd make it through the night, whether they'd be able to stay on the hull that long, and what would happen if there was another thunderstorm. They were common this time of year.

Then a few miles to the west Paul saw a light low in the sky that he thought might be a helicopter. The light moved north a few miles, maybe to the edge of the sound, then went back south. Eventually it turned and went north again.

He didn't mention it at first, as if he'd jinx it by saying aloud that it was running a search pattern. But it kept going back and forth along a line a long way to the west of them. Then Karen spotted it too. Was it getting closer? They couldn't tell.

Then it disappeared.

Sometime later it was back, traversing the same route back and forth. Now it looked closer. Paul pushed the button on his watch to illuminate its face: almost midnight. They'd been out here for almost 8 hours.

Back and forth. Back and forth. Now they could hear its chopping blades in the distance. Yes—closer!

But by 1 A.M. it still seemed far away. Paul was worried: Karen was shivering hard and her voice was getting shaky; what if she slipped back into the water? They should have kept jackets or something in the boat cubby, he thought. He moved closer to her on the hull and carefully worked his arm around her to warm her.

Back and forth. As the helicopter banked in its turn Paul caught a flash of light, a searchlight being played over the water. They *were* searching!

Soon they could see it really was coming closer, although painfully slowly. The searchlight swung back and forth as the craft flew its straight lines.

"They'll be here soon," he said at last, silently praying they wouldn't have to turn back for more fuel first.

Finally they could actually see the searchlight on the water as the helicopter passed and again flew on to its northern turning point. Back it came, now almost directly overhead, and the light flashed on their upturned faces, blinding them. But then it passed over them and went on. He heard Karen gasp in dismay.

But the light was back almost immediately, and stayed on them. They had to look away from the bright light but waved frantically. They heard the engine grow louder as the helicopter descended and hovered.

Very soon a Coast Guard swimmer came down a cable with a rescue basket and, after checking their condition, radioed the pilot and helped Karen into the basket. He assured Paul a boat was almost there and then ascended with Karen. The helicopter remained at hover until a fast cutter arrived a minute later and took Paul aboard.

"You can thank your neighbor for this," the guardsman told him then. "He saw you go out this afternoon and not come back. He called us around eight o'clock and we've been searching ever since, but we thought you were a long way west of here. Lots of water to cover."

Paul nodded, adding another item to his mental to-do list.

Later, as the cutter motored back toward the Coast Guard station, they radioed in and then told him that Karen had been checked and was just fine. "Pretty lucky, you two," the guardsman added.

The Inverted Cat

Day 1

He could not believe the sun would set on him out here, was setting. All afternoon Juan had sat precariously on the catamaran's inverted hull, legs in the water, watching one horizon, then another. He mostly watched to the east, back toward Culebra, waiting for a fishing boat to pass by and see him. There should have been dozens of boats by now, not just one or two on the far horizon headed he knew not where. The boats going back to Fajardo should have come right by him.

What scared him most was that Culebra had disappeared sometime in the afternoon, just slipped away as if the island had sunk into the sea. Without its smudge on the horizon he felt disoriented. Not until the sun was dropping could he even figure out directions. How can an island just disappear? But he knew he was not crazy, that he had to be moving away for the island to disappear, but with the boat turned turtle and the mast and sail in the water like a giant sea anchor, it should not have been blown far. Besides, the wind was very light now and had been most of the day, once the morning squall had passed, that gusty squall that had flipped the Hobie only an hour into his sail.

His mother was going to kill him. She'd ordered him not to try this crossing in his little boat, but he was old enough now to decide for himself and had just smiled at her fear and told her he was spending the weekend with friends.

Again he tried to calculate the distances. It was about 30 kilometers from Culebra to Fajardo, just an adventurous trade-wind sail of only 4 hours or so. Had he sailed maybe 8 kilometers before the squall struck? Until near the end he was sailing the compass course of 290 degrees. When the squall struck the wind abruptly went south, then southeast, and he had hauled in the sheets tight and shot forward like a rocket, until that gust.

Next time, he kept telling himself, repeating the phrase all day like a mantra, next time he would tie a lanyard on the compass. Thankfully his water bottle floated and had bobbed up close by where he could swim to it, but he had lost everything else. He had dived under and found the boat bag still tied to the trapeze, but everything had spilled out: his watch, his cell phone, the sunscreen, his lunch . . . and his compass.

Next time, too, he would repair the broken mast float so the boat wouldn't turn turtle and he could right it as he had been taught long ago.

When the sun was gone, he had a moment of fear and raised his legs as far as he could from the water, but it was difficult to balance with only the rudder to hold on to and eventually he put them back in the water. Where were the boats? Where was the island?

Day 2

He should not have drunk so much of his water yesterday. He had been so sure a boat would pass soon. Now he had only a little left, and by midmorning the hot sun was drying his sweat almost as soon as it appeared and his mouth was dry cotton. He took a sip only occasionally, but each time the water seemed to soak into his tongue and cheeks before he could swallow. His dry throat ached.

His mind was getting fuzzy, too, but that was probably from the heat and lack of sleep through the longest night of his life. The stars had been so bright they made his eyes sore. All night he kept reminding himself to keep watch. There was nothing on the horizon where Culebra should be, judging direction from the swell, and the distant sky glow that ought to be Fajardo was not quite where it should be either.

Sometimes he thought there were lights of boats on the horizon, but usually they were just stars that rose brighter or dropped into the ocean.

He was so thirsty. He stared into the sea and thought of water, his thoughts drifting, and then he would jerk out of his fog and remember to look around again.

The sun was very high when he found himself staring at his arms, noticing he wasn't sweating. That seemed odd. He touched the skin and pulled his hand back; it was hotter than he felt on the inside.

With both hands firmly grasping the rudder that pointed absurdly at the sky, he slipped off the hull into the water, easing

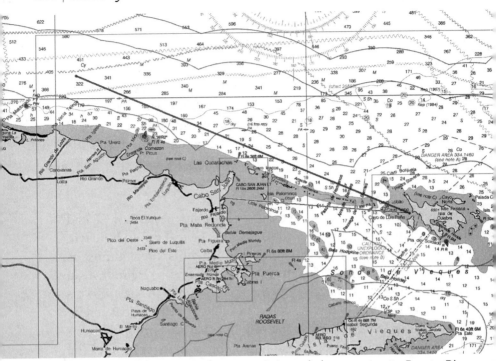

Chart section showing the catamaran's intended course west to Puerto Rico and how it drifted to the northwest in the current.

in down to his neck. The cool water felt wonderful. A little wave slapped his face and wet his lips, and his tongue went out to lick them—but he caught himself in time. Drinking salt water kills you; first it makes you crazy and then it kills you.

He thought again of the canvas boat bag beneath the catamaran. Maybe he should check it again for his compass. Maybe it was wedged in a fold at the bottom and he had missed it yesterday.

Then he got angry at himself. What good was a compass? He was not going anywhere.

He realized that with his eyes so low to the water he could not see far, and then only for a moment on each wave crest. He had to get higher to see farther. But he did not want to get back out in the sun.

Maybe he should try again to right the catamaran. There must be something more that he could try. By himself he was not heavy enough to push one hull far enough down to lever the other up. Think! But he could not think of how, and he was too tired to make the effort.

He climbed out and crouched as high as he could on the hull, balancing with one hand on the rudder, and looked around.

Back in the water. Back up to look. The last of his water was long gone. A dull lethargy settled in, his thoughts drifting, until suddenly he would remember to look again.

He saw boats sometimes, a long way off. Late in the day a big sport fisherman with a high flying bridge seemed closer and he tried to stand to his full height and wave his arms, but he slipped and fell into the water. Stupid! he tried to shout at himself, hearing only a dry croak that startled him. But it made him realize he needed some way to signal a passing boat. He thought for a while, then dived under the boat and removed the tiller extension to use as a pole that he could tie his shirt to. It took him several attempts to get it free, but eventually he sat again on the hull with the pole across his lap, panting, his head aching, but feeling more hopeful for a time. He looked for boats again.

Then the sun went down.

Day 3

During the night he had strange thoughts and wondered if he was asleep and dreaming of stars or was still awake. How could he tell the difference? When the first light of dawn showed him the sea around him, at first he wasn't sure where he was.

He found the tiller extension pole still wedged tightly through his belt and stared at it. What was that doing there?

He was beyond thirst now, his mouth a clot and his lips stuck together, though he thought of water continually in an abstract way. Like the sea. Like boats. Like the sun. All just vague abstractions. He numbly went in and out of the water to stay cool, but he had all but forgotten why he got back out.

This last time he had great difficulty climbing out, and he felt dizzy as soon as he sat up. His head throbbed with a fast beat, and his heart raced in his ears and throat. Nausea and cramps bent him double; he just wanted to drop back into the water.

Maybe he could tie himself to the hull with his belt and close his eyes for a while.

Maybe he could just let go and drift away peacefully. But he did not feel peaceful. He felt dizzy, sick, and angry.

Then the sun went down.

Midnight

He dreamed of being lost in the stars, swimming in the Milky Way. The stars were bright all around him, and the giant moon at his side was so bright he narrowed his eyes. He heard music above the slapping waves, music like heaven. The moon was so close he could touch it.

He raised one hand toward the moon and saw it silhouetted in the light, many lights all along the water, lights between his spread fingers. He felt a deep throbbing in the water as if his heart had swollen and was beating so fast it was a continual thrumming. The sound grew suddenly louder and startled him, and then his eyes focused and he saw row after row of lights past his hand—a ship!

It was approaching obliquely, a massive ship, so lit up it looked like a ship of souls bound for heaven. Then recognition: it was a cruise ship. Coming almost right at him!

Adrenaline shot through him as he ripped off his shirt and hastily tied it to the pole and began waving it as high as he could. Surely they would see him; the ship was so close he was bathed in its light. He saw shapes of people behind the windows.

He tried to shout but his throat was too dry. He cupped a hand in the sea and splashed it into his mouth, then spat. "Help!" he screamed into the roar of passing engines. He waved his shirt frantically and searched the empty deck rail for someone to see him.

As the ship passed he slipped and fell back in the water. By the time he climbed back up and discovered he had lost the pole with his shirt, it was already moving away.

The stars all went out as the music faded.

Much later, they told him it had been only another hour before the helicopter found him, but he had no memory of it. They said he looked straight up into the searchlight but did not wave, did not even move his mouth or blink. Where had he been?

He did not remember the helicopter and only barely recalled the rescue boat. What he remembered best was waking in the hospital and being given a single ice chip to suck on.

You were very lucky, they told him still later. A passenger saw you as the ship passed, but no one believed him until they reviewed the security camera tapes, which showed a quick flicker in the dark waves. By then it was too late to turn back, but the captain radioed the Coast Guard.

They showed him the chart and where they had found him, 8 kilometers north of Loiza. Loiza! That was 30 kilometers beyond Fajardo and far to the north, over 50 kilometers from where he had capsized.

"The current," they told him. In a week he might have washed up in the Bahamas. He had been very lucky.

Briefly

Hog Neck Bay, New York, August 2011. A brother and sister in their early twenties were sailing their Sunfish offshore when it capsized. They were wearing life jackets and stayed afloat but were unable to right the boat. They had no way to call for help. They stayed with the overturned hull for a time but eventually decided the odds were against anyone happening upon them. Although they were at least 2 miles from shore, they set off swimming. Soon they were exhausted and cold, but good luck was with them. Their mother had gotten worried and called the police. They were found still a mile and a half offshore.

Lake Huron, Michigan, March 2010. The Coast Guard always urges boaters to carry a VHF radio rather than a cell phone in case of an emergency, but these three girls, ages 12 and 13, apparently weren't thinking much about safety issues when they "borrowed" a small sailboat from the beach and went out on Lake Huron without PFDs or oars. They were blown a mile into the frigid lake and were unable to sail back. Lucky that her cell phone was still dry, the 13-year-old called 911 for help moments before the boat capsized on a wave and her wet phone died. They clung to the capsized hull and were rescued before hypothermia set in.

Little Sister Bay, Wisconsin, June 2007. A solo sailor capsized and stayed with his boat as long as he could, but he had no way to call for help. No one saw him or the boat. The next day his granddaughter reported him missing, and the following day another boater discovered and reported his overturned boat. His body was later found.

York River, Yorktown, Virginia, July 2012. Two sailors in a 14-foot sailboat capsized while sailing on the York River. They wore life jackets and clung to the overturned boat, but they were scared to try swimming the distance to shore and had no way to call for help. By chance, a Coast Guardsman from the West Coast, who had been attending a search-and-rescue school in Yorktown, was riding his bicycle along the river at dusk when he spotted the capsized sailboat and quickly telephoned for help. They were rescued before dark as a result of the kind of luck we all hope for but can scarcely expect.

St. Petersburg, Florida, February 2012. Two men in their mid-twenties were sailing a 16-foot Hobie Cat off Pinellas Point when the boat capsized on a gust. They were unable to right the catamaran, and there were no other boats nearby to hail for help. They did have a submersible handheld VHF radio and were able to call the Coast Guard on channel 16. Twenty-five minutes later a rescue boat arrived, took the two aboard, and towed the Hobie back to port.

CHAPTER 9

A Thousand Ways to End Up in the Water

W*hen boaters are asked in surveys about their use of PFDs, the largest group answers "Sometimes." A minority always wear one and a few admit to never using one, but most feel confident they will be able to put one on when conditions worsen. Still, statistics reveal the huge majority of boating fatalities involve drownings when the person was not wearing a life jacket, suggesting he or she had little fear of suddenly ending up in the water. But even in calm conditions—the time most fatalities occur—there are a thousand ways to unexpectedly end up in the water.*

To Save a Puppy

From the day they'd rescued Pepper, a mixed-breed puppy, from the local pound, Nick and Pepper were inseparable, to the point that Nick's father, Scott, worried Nick wasn't even trying to make friends at his new school. Every day Nick rushed home from middle school to play with the puppy in their backyard in a Houston suburb. It's just a phase he's going through, Scott told himself. Sooner or later he'll find other interests and start making friends. But for now the most they could get Nick to do was take weekly swimming lessons at the local pool, and he'd gotten pretty good at it. As a bonus, he seemed to really enjoy the water.

On Saturday morning when Scott suggested they go for a sail at a nearby lake, he asked Nick if he wanted to ask a friend to come along.

"Can I bring Pepper instead?" the boy asked.

Scott sighed. "I guess so," he said at last. "As long as you take care of him. I'll be busy with the boat."

Nick grinned. "Of course I will!"

It was a sunny day with light winds, a perfect day for an easy sail around the lake. Too bad his wife had to work, because she enjoyed sailing as much as he did. In fact, she was the one who had talked him into buying their used sailboat earlier in the spring.

He made sandwiches, packed a cooler, and hitched the trailer to his pickup, and they set off for the lake.

While Scott launched the boat, Nick and Pepper ran around on the shore. "Think I can teach Pepper to swim?" Nick called.

"Most dogs figure it out on their own."

"I know, I can teach him to dog-paddle!" Nick shouted. He threw a stick in the water, but Pepper stopped at the water's edge.

"Maybe when he's bigger," Scott said.

When the 14-foot daysailer was rigged and tied up to the dock alongside the boat ramp, they stowed their gear and Nick put Pepper in the cockpit. Scott surveyed the treetops along shore, looking for wind. They'd have to stay close in, he thought, in case the light breeze died; otherwise it would be a slow trip back. They'd never been becalmed out on the lake before, but he'd been thinking about buying a trolling motor for the boat just in case they were. He should get some life jackets too.

Once they'd ghosted a few hundred yards from shore, the wind was better and soon they were sailing along just fine on a beam reach.

After a while Pepper got used to the boat and was trying to explore, climbing up onto the cockpit seats. "Better keep a hand on him," Scott told Nick. "He's still young and foolish."

Nick tried to keep the puppy on his lap and hold on to the

cockpit coaming at the same time. Pepper was just big enough to be hard to control with one hand.

Near the center of the mile-wide lake, Scott turned the boat to sail downwind, letting out the sails. As he'd learned, he raised the centerboard to reduce drag. As he was adjusting the sails he caught movement in the corner of his eye and turned to see Pepper claw free from Nick's grasp, haul himself over the coaming, and promptly topple overboard with a splash.

"Dad!"

Nick had stood up and was reaching for the puppy, but already the boat had moved on.

"I'll get him!" Nick said and stood on the seat.

"Wait!" Scott said, but Nick had already jumped in.

Scott froze for several seconds, watching. His first impulse was to jump in after Nick, but the boat was moving steadily away and it might be tough to swim back to it. He scanned the water all around; there was only one fishing boat against the far shore, too far away to hear him shout. He looked back to Nick, who had easily swum to Pepper and seemed to be treading water okay. "Got him, Dad!" he yelled.

So Scott sat back down, swung the tiller over all the way, and began trimming in the sails to return to Nick. The problem, he saw immediately, was that Nick was directly upwind; he would have to tack back.

The boat felt infuriatingly slow but at least it was moving, although not as much in the right direction as he wanted it to. He looked at Nick, who was trying to hold Pepper out of the water some 40 yards away, apparently treading water with just his legs.

The sailboat was being blown sideways as it angled back, so he turned the tiller more and hauled the sheets tighter, almost stalling the boat. Then he remembered the centerboard was still up.

"Dad! Help!" Nick shouted.

He looked and saw Nick splashing but couldn't tell exactly what was happening.

Quickly he locked the helm with one knee over the tiller and fumbled with the centerboard line. The board hung up for a moment, then went down, and he checked that the sails were still drawing and got a hand back on the tiller to try to head up. The boat was moving better now. Nick was still splashing. Another minute and he could tack, then a minute more and he'd reach Nick, still faster than he could swim to him.

He couldn't stand the wait. He pushed the tiller across, and the bow swung slowly over and into the wind. He let the jib back for a moment to help blow the bow across, then quickly released the sheet and hauled in the other.

He was watching ahead as the bow fell off onto the other tack, but he couldn't see Nick where he thought he should be. He stood and surveyed the water all about—nothing.

He dropped the tiller and jumped to the cockpit seat to dive in, then caught himself. If the boat got away, they'd both drown. He looked around, sighted against a tall tree on the distant shore to calculate his position, and then rushed to the mast and released both halyards. The sails rattled down, and he dived into the water and swam toward the tree.

As he swam and dived, feeling his way through murky water, his mind rejected the situation. Nick could not simply have vanished like that; he'd pop up somewhere nearby any moment.

He searched until he was so exhausted he was barely able to get back to the drifting boat. Part of him didn't want to.

Once back on shore he telephoned for help from the truck, and the water-rescue people arrived quickly. They wouldn't let him on the boat when they went out in the direction he pointed. The light breeze had all but died, and the waves were very small and wouldn't conceal anything floating. He sat on the shore, dazed, watching.

When they came back later, he saw right away they had the dead puppy. Then they opened a plastic bag and showed him a pair of sneakers they'd found floating. He recognized them and nodded, and they put the bag away.

"We have a diver on the way," they told him.

By dark the diver had found nothing. Numb, Scott still couldn't accept it, still expected Nick to come walking up along the shore from where he'd swum out. He'd have to tell the boy he could get a new dog.

Three days later a fisherman found Nick's floating body.

Gone Fishing

"Three old farts on a boat," Scully's wife called them. Well, maybe the other two, Scully thought, since Nolan and Geoff were both older and retired. He was just between jobs; it wasn't his fault the older guys were his only friends free to sail on a weekday.

"Your unemployment's going to run out soon," his wife reminded Scully again in the morning when he told her they were taking the boat out on Long Island Sound.

"All the more reason to enjoy it while I can," he told her. "Besides, I'll bring home fish for dinner. Some blues, maybe a striper."

"Like that will pay for the beer," she said, watching him pack ice around the case in the big cooler.

But she smiled. She didn't really begrudge him his time on the water. It seemed about the only thing he enjoyed these days.

Scully picked up Nolan and Geoff at their houses on the way to the marina where his 22-foot pocket cruiser was docked. When the checks stopped he'd have to keep it at home on its trailer, but until then he planned to enjoy the marina's convenience as often as possible.

"We headin' toward Fishers?" Nolan asked.

"I heard the blues are running," Geoff added.

"That's the plan," Scully said. "Wind's supposed to be light, just right for sailing at trolling speed." He glanced into the back seat at the pile of stuff they'd brought along. "One of you old farts remember sandwiches?"

Nolan and Geoff looked at each other and broke out laughing. From the back seat Geoff twisted around and lifted the lid of the cooler in back. "Doesn't look like much room in here for sandwiches, anyway. Sure you got enough beer?"

Scully snorted. "It's gonna be hot this afternoon, trust me. I'll sell 'em to you a buck a can and you'll be begging for more."

"Okay," Nolan sighed. "Stop somewhere and I'll pay for the sandwiches."

"I'll kick in for gas," Geoff offered. "So's you don't keep calling me old fart."

It was after 11 A.M. by the time they parked at the marina and loaded everything into Scully's old sloop.

"Geez, ever think of hosing this thing off once in a while?" Nolan said, surveying the deck.

"That's what rain's for." Scully unscrewed the cap of the outboard gas tank with its busted gauge and looked inside. "Got enough gas, so you can kick in for the beer," he told Geoff. "Put that cooler down below out of the sun."

"Pretty hot already," Nolan said.

"Have a beer, then."

They opened three cans, and Scully set to work starting the old Johnson two-stroke outboard. As usually happened, his arm got tired from pulling the cord and the thing had only coughed a couple times.

"It's that ethanol," Geoff said. "Gums up the carb on old motors."

"Thanks," Scully said. "Real helpful."

Finally the outboard started with a big puff of blue smoke.

"Let's get out on the river before it dies again," Nolan said. "Tide's runnin' out, right?"

Geoff untied the lines and Scully backed out of the slip, keeping up the rpm. When he shifted into forward with a roar, the boat lurched and Nolan, who was still stowing gear, dropped his beer and almost fell over.

They watched the foamy liquid swirl down the cockpit drain as they cleared the last floating dock and turned down the Thames River through New London Harbor for the 3-mile run out into Long Island Sound.

"Get me another beer," Scully said, "and get that sail cover off." He was hot already, the cooler breeze of the sound still far ahead.

Geoff rigged a lure and cast far out to port. "Won't catch anything in here," Nolan said.

"You never know."

"Well, for all that," Scully said, settled back on his cushion, "you never know about nothin'."

"Ain't that the truth."

An hour later the harbor mouth had widened out and the boat was rising and falling on lazy swells rolling in from the sound. The air was cooler now but not much. Through the haze ahead they could see the western end of Fishers Island. When they cleared the last of the inshore ledges Scully directed them to raise the sails and then shut off the noisy outboard.

"Ah, the quiet!" he exclaimed. "It's what I live for these days."

"I'll drink to that."

The wind was about 8 knots west-southwest, letting Scully sail on a beam reach toward Fishers. They had two lines in the water, Nolan and Geoff holding the rods out to either side. Scully watched the sails and the tips of the rods. It was a fine day, and it wouldn't matter much if they never got a bite, though he'd like to take home a couple of fish for his wife.

The afternoon got hotter as the wind dropped. They turned east through Fishers Sound, passing the Dumplings, sailing downwind now, just ghosting along. The problem with downwind sailing, though, was that you felt no breeze at all and there was no shade from the sails. Fortunately they had lots of cold beer.

After a while Geoff went down in the cabin to take a nap. Nolan looked at his line and said, "It's just hanging straight down," and reeled it in.

Scully decided to turn for the slow sail back. At this rate it might take until dark.

But there wasn't enough wind to move forward against the tide through the sound. "Screw it," he said at last. "Let's motor-sail a while."

But the outboard wouldn't start, and pretty soon both his and Nolan's arms were tired from pulling the cord.

"Get me my toolbox," Scully said.

Nolan climbed below and found the toolbox. "It's cooler down there in the shade," he said. "You need my help with the motor?"

"Nah, I'm just gonna clean the plug, check the fuel filter."

"I think I'll lie down for a while, then," Nolan said. "Get out of the sun."

"Get me a beer first."

Scully opened the toolbox and spread out some tools on the cockpit seat. Then he bent over the transom to the outboard on its low mount and worked off the top cover. Getting to the motor from the cockpit was a real bitch. It didn't fit on the small mount well and couldn't be rotated around to make it easier. To reach the spark plug to the rear, he practically had to lie prone with his legs on the bench seat, his stomach pressed uncomfortably against the aft cockpit wall, and then reach way out and around, feeling with his fingers—all without dropping the wrench in the water. What a hassle!

He got the plug out and wormed back into the cockpit. It looked pretty dirty and was oily at the tip. He wiped it with a rag, then brushed it off with a wire brush and checked the gap.

He drank the rest of his beer and squinted up at the sun. Then he moved some tools out of his way and crawled back out over the transom with the plug and wrench.

Just as he was working the plug back in, fumbling with the wrench, he felt his sunglasses slipping off. With his other hand he let go of the transom to grab them before they fell.

Neither Geoff nor Nolan had any idea how long they'd slept. Geoff woke first, groggy, and climbed out the companionway to look around. The sun was lower but it was still hot, and the boat bobbed in the low swells without wind. He looked around the boat and took in the tools spread over the cockpit seat.

"Hey, Nolan, where's Scully?" he yelled back down the companionway.

Nolan was slow to wake. "What?"

"Where'd Scully go?"

He rubbed his eyes. "What do you mean, where'd he go?"

"He's not here."

Nolan climbed out, and together they looked all around the boat and scanned the water.

"Some kind of joke?" They looked at each other. "Like he got off on another boat?"

But they knew Scully wouldn't do that. There was no explanation, he was just gone. Geoff moved back and looked at the open outboard. "He was going to check the plug," Nolan said. "That's what he was doing when I went below."

Then it occurred to them that maybe he'd fallen overboard and that they should do something. Geoff took out his cell phone and looked at Nolan. "What am I supposed to say?"

● ● ● — — — ● ● ●

Scully's body was found 3 days later. There was no sign of injury, and he was not wearing a life jacket. The autopsy showed he had drowned, and it was presumed he'd fallen overboard and become separated from the boat.

Briefly

The Mediterranean, October 2011. French sailor Florence Arthaud, famed solo sailor, was sailing singlehanded off the coast of France. Like many sailors she likely knew the more-than-half-true Coast Guard joke that drowned (male) boaters are always found with their zipper down, the result of falling in while urinating overboard. (This is actually more true of powerboaters, who lack stays, shrouds, and lifelines to grab as needed.) But she was apparently not thinking about this when one night, as she later said, she was "having a tinkle over the rail without attaching myself as usual" and was unluckily bounced overboard by a wave. Luckily, however, she'd just bought a waterproof case for her cell phone before starting the voyage, and luckily the phone had a signal. She got a call through and was found in the dark after an hour and a half suffering from hypothermia, but was released from the hospital later without harm.

A lake in Utah, 2008. A father and his two sons were sailing a small boat that capsized when the wind and waves increased. None of them wore a PFD. They succeeded in righting the boat and getting back in, but one of the boys noticed their paddle was floating away and jumped back in to retrieve it. The wind was blowing the boat away from him faster than he could swim back, so his father jumped in the water with a line to try to reach his son. He couldn't get to him, so he returned to the boat to help his other son sail back to the boy in the water. They watched as he took off his shoes in order to swim better, but he disappeared under the surface before they could reach him. The recovery search was fruitless; his body was found when it surfaced 4 days later.

Phuket, Thailand, February 2012. An Australian woman was sailing offshore near Phuket with three other experienced sailors on a large cruising sailboat when she mysteriously disappeared at night when on deck alone. The others had no idea what happened or exactly when it happened during her watch, but they assumed she had fallen overboard. The extensive search operation turned up nothing. They could only imagine her horror as, alone in the water in the dark, she helplessly watched the boat sail away.

Lake Champlain, Vermont, 2007. Two people were sailing on the lake when one accidentally dropped a winch handle overboard. It was a warm day and he could swim, so he thought nothing of jumping in to fetch the floating handle. Without a PFD, however, he was unable to stay on the surface long enough for the other person to sail the boat back. Twelve days passed before his body was found.

Lake Michigan, Indiana, 2009. A husband and wife were out on their sailboat on a hot, windless day and decided to cool off by swimming beside the boat. The boat drifted off, and soon the man was struggling in the water. His wife tried to hold up his head, but by the time rescuers arrived he'd been facedown in the water for 30 minutes and could not be resuscitated.

Lake Erie, Presque Isle, Pennsylvania, July 2011. A small group was sailing 2 hours before sunset when one of them, a 27-year-old man, jumped in for a swim. When the others saw him struggling in the 78°F water, they threw him a life ring, but he couldn't reach it and soon went under. They called for help and a Coast Guard boat arrived within minutes, but rescuers were unable to find him.

San Diego Bay, California, March 2011. There were ten people aboard the 26-foot water-ballasted sailboat when it capsized, likely because the boat was overloaded and the passengers' weight was poorly distributed. Two men, ages 44 and 73, who were not wearing life jackets, drowned despite the immediate response of good Samaritans nearby and professional rescuers who were soon on the scene. The other eight people on board were rescued, some of whom had worn PFDs, and seven were taken to area hospitals; all survived. Investigators later commented that the boat contained life jackets that were not being used and, incidentally, that the mainsail was held together with duct tape and staples.

James River, Virginia, May 2011. Ten people in their twenties decided to cruise the broad coastal river on a 22-foot centerboard sailboat at midnight, following a party. For unclear reasons the boat capsized, throwing them all in the water. No one was wearing a life jacket. Five managed to swim several miles to shore, and three others clung to floating debris until they were rescued. Two drowned.

Lake Arthur, Pennsylvania, July 2010. A husband and wife were sailing their 22-foot sailboat when he decided to go for a swim. The boat began to drift away, and his wife tried to throw him a Type IV PFD, but he couldn't reach it. He called to her for help, but she didn't know how to start the boat's engine or work the sails. She shouted to a nearby boat for help, which responded and got him aboard. Despite CPR on the boat and professional treatment by paramedics on shore and physicians later at the hospital, he did not survive.

Flathead Lake, Montana, September 2011. While sailing with friends, a 57-year-old man jumped in the water for a swim. After a time he was struggling to stay afloat. The others successfully turned the boat around and eventually got back to him and got him aboard, but he could not be revived.

CHAPTER 10

The Perils of Solo Sailing

*S*ome sail only with friends or crew, or singlehandedly only
*reluctantly, while others actively enjoy sailing solo and the
heightened feelings of competence and self-sufficiency it
brings. For most experienced sailors, solo sailing on an appropri-
ately equipped boat is no more dangerous than sailing with crew
as long as they take precautions, such as using a tether to prevent
falling overboard and having other safety and communications
gear at hand. But some solo sailors, like some sailors with crew,
seem either not to have thought about the inherent risks or to feel
some certainty that disaster can't happen to them. In many cases
when a singlehanded sailing incident results in a fatality, there are
no witnesses and we can only imagine what may have happened.
But like almost all sailing disasters, these incidents could have been
prevented or resolved successfully if only the sailor had considered
everything that can happen and taken appropriate steps—especially
important when sailing solo.*

A Sailboat Comes Ashore

It was another nice Southern California day in September, a good
day for sailing, when Jason decided to go fishing along the coast.
He had his fishing gear on his 24-foot sloop, on which he had been
living part-time since separating from his wife. All he needed to
do was top off the fuel tank on his way out of the marina.

At age 57, sailing and fishing were Jason's main passions, and either could make up for the other if they both weren't great. Today he was optimistic; the forecast was a perfect 10 to 15 knots of wind, medium swells, and sunny. Maybe the fish would be biting too. If not, the sailing would be enough to keep his mind off his troubles.

It was noon when he motored out of the Redondo Beach marina on a southerly breeze. With the engine still running and the autopilot engaged, he turned south into the wind to raise the mainsail, and then fell off the wind some 50 degrees and unfurled the jib. Then he reset the autopilot to sail due west, out to sea, on a comfortable beam reach.

While he enjoyed fishing, Jason had to admit he wasn't very scientific about it, and he chose his location and course more for the sailing than for the fishing. He seldom messed with live bait but had an assortment of lures and plastic squid in a variety of colors, and usually he'd just troll a long line from a rod lashed to a stern stanchion and see what happened. It was probably too late in the season for white sea bass, but there was always a chance of happening upon a halibut or even a yellowtail.

He chose a yellow squid and cast, letting the boat's movement carry out the line. He set the drag at medium so he'd hear it if a fish took the lure. Then he trimmed the mainsail and furled in the jib a few wraps so the boat wouldn't be going too fast if he got a strike. In the past he'd tried to stop the boat when he had a fish by heaving-to or stalling out into the wind, but that usually caused trouble if the fish ran one way or the other, and he would have to climb all over the boat to keep the line from wrapping the keel, prop, or rudder. Now he just kept on sailing, sometimes easing the sheets to spill wind and slow down, and tried to keep the boat moving forward and the fish off the stern. It was harder to reel in against the movement, but at least the line stayed behind the boat most of the time.

Nothing was happening. After an hour he changed course so he was close-hauled to the southwest as he ate lunch, and then went to a broad reach back to the northwest. He was now several miles offshore, the Los Angeles coastline a distant blur of haze and smog. At three o'clock he jibed around to an easterly course to jog back toward shore. Then—finally!—at about four thirty the rod tip jerked and the line started out, the drag singing.

He glanced quickly at the autopilot and sails, then grabbed the rod and began playing the fish. It felt big, or at least feisty. It turned in and ran sometimes and he'd reel in furiously, but then it turned again and he had to give up line. No way he could put the rod down now to slow the boat, he had to keep playing the fish.

It jumped once about 50 feet back; it was a barracuda, and a big one! Not good for eating, but fun to wrestle with. It seemed to take forever to wear down this monster and get it to the side of the boat. Jason crouched on his knees on the cockpit seat and reached down with the net. Now the barracuda came back alive, kicking. It was hard to control the rod with one hand and the net with the other; the fish was just too big and fast, jaws open and teeth flashing. Finally it held still right at the surface, and Jason leaned out farther, reaching down, and had just about netted the fish when it jerked the rod again and he lost his balance and tumbled off the boat.

His first thought after the shock of cold water was the barracuda —where was it? He'd dropped the net and now quickly released the rod, hoping the barracuda with its rows of razor-sharp teeth would swim away. He spun around as he treaded water, looking for the fish.

Then he saw his sailboat sailing away. Immediately he started swimming hard, pulling with long strokes, head down, not worrying about breathing, racing wildly to try to catch up. When at last he had to bring his face up for air, he saw the boat was farther away still, sails full and well trimmed, leaving a straight-line wake as it sailed east. He forced himself to stop and relax, treading water slowly.

He started thinking, calmer now. He studied the coastline when a swell lifted him; it was at least 2 miles away, maybe 3.

Could he swim that far? Yes, he was sure of it, because he was good at floating on his back and could take a break whenever he got tired. He'd make it, he was sure. He kicked off his shoes in order to swim better.

But he was so cold.

••• — — —•••

At five o'clock the bar at Old Tony's on the Redondo Beach pier was just starting to fill up, a few tourists tired of shopping and the first locals off work early. It was a favorite spot for watching people on the pier and boats passing nearby. Sunlight glistened off the water, and the sails were prettily backlit by the orange sun. In the distance a small sloop was coming in toward one of the marinas just north of the pier. As it approached on a beam reach, a sailor at the bar approvingly noted its straight wake. He sipped his beer, watching, waiting for the inevitable swing north for the marina.

••• — — —•••

Jason set his mind on making a thousand strokes and counted to himself, trying to breathe regularly. As long as he kept swimming, the cold was not as bad. But at number 290 he had to pause to rest, and then the cold squeezed him like a vise. He wasn't in as good a shape as he'd once been. Floating for a minute, trying to relax and stop shivering, he suddenly wondered if there was an ocean current here. From a swell top he checked the shore, which looked no closer, and thought maybe he was being swept off course. With a spurt of panic he started swimming again, trying to pace himself, trying to relax his muscles.

••• — — —•••

What the hell? The sailor at the bar watched the sloop approaching the section of the pier broadside to the waves. It should have turned by now, even if the sailors on board were "buzzing" the tourists on the pier. The helmsman was cutting it pretty close. He stood and walked to the window. The sloop's hull disappeared from sight below the angle of the pier, but the masthead came straight on. He turned and ran down the stairs and out the door that opened out on to the pier and sprinted down the pier. Then he heard the metallic crash of the mast and saw the masthead with its wind vane swinging wildly as the hull bashed against the pylons below. He reached the rail and looked down at the boat but could see no one on deck. He took out his cell phone and punched in the three digits.

••• — — —•••

Now it was occurring to Jason that he might not make it after all. It was like his body had a will of its own and just wanted to stop moving and sink. He had to force his arms and legs to take each stroke. If he stopped to rest, he might not be able to get started again. One stroke, then another. He was thinking of his elderly mother, who expected him for dinner tonight. How long would it take before someone called her?

••• — — —•••

The city police arrived first, the harbor patrol a minute later by boat. They quickly checked the sloop. Men in uniform on the pier and men in the boat below were busy on their radios. The sailor from the bar watched a while from the periphery, then stood looking at the long glare of the orange-red sun on the water to the west. Somewhere out there, he couldn't help thinking, there was somebody without a boat. He shuddered at the thought of it. Then he heard the sound of a helicopter and saw one of the lifeguard choppers rushing down the shore from the north. It reached the pier and hovered a moment, then continued south just offshore.

••• — — —•••

For some reason it was easier to swim with his eyes closed, as if not seeing the distant shore made it closer, more possible. But once when he opened his eyes again, as he fought to keep moving in a slow crawl, he saw the sun low in front of him, and the shock of that snapped alert him as if from a dream. He turned east again, grimly opening his eyes when he raised his head to breathe. It wouldn't be long until dark, he thought, when it would feel natural just to go to sleep.

•• — — —•••

The Coast Guard helicopter, its crew better trained for search and rescue, took over the air search and started a grid pattern. A half-dozen watercraft went west into the ocean to search. The lifeguard helicopter stayed low to sweep the beach areas north and south. The radio had informed the searchers that the police had traced the boat by its registration numbers and spoken to someone at the marina who had seen the boat leave with just one man aboard.

••• — — —•••

It was almost dark now, and he knew some sort of end would be coming. The sun was down, the sky behind him a fading red. He took a slow stroke, grabbed air, paused a few seconds, tried to stroke again. The stars were coming out now, one star at least. Low in the sky to the east. It was moving, or maybe he was moving, he couldn't tell anymore. Just one lonely star in the sky and him in the water. It seemed sad. Then he choked, gasped, threw up his head and coughed out water. He'd let his head go under with his mouth open. There was that star again. He tried to swim toward it but found he couldn't move his arms anymore.

••• — — —•••

With its bright searchlight, the helicopter continued its grid search, now about 2 miles offshore. It had been almost 3 hours since the sailboat had crashed into the pier. Though no one said it, the four crew on board were thinking of the effects of hypothermia on anyone in the water. The water was just too cold. Hopefully the guy in the water was wearing a PFD that kept his head up even if he was unconscious. They were thinking too that if he'd been in a dinghy or life raft, they should've spotted him already, unless he was way out in the Pacific somewhere. So he was likely in the water and would be nearly impossible to see.

About eight o'clock they spotted someone floating in the water below. Not moving, apparently not wearing a PFD, face-down in the water. They radioed the nearest rescue boat, which could reach the person sooner than their rescue swimmer, and in less than a minute the boat's crew were bringing the man on deck. The radio crackled; someone thought they felt a weak pulse. The boat shot off for shore at top speed.

It was only a matter of minutes before Jason was transferred to paramedics in an ambulance and rushed to the hospital, CPR continuing the whole way. But at 8:15, as the last of twilight faded, Jason was pronounced dead.

The Fouled Halyard

Zimmerman was sitting in the cockpit of his Catalina 30 sailboat on the outer dock of the Manatee River marina enjoying a mid-morning cup of coffee when he heard a sputtering outboard out on the broad river. He turned to look; yep, it was that older guy, Wylie, or whatever his name was, puttering about in his open day-sailer. He was a couple hundred yards from shore, moving slowly down away from the bridge, no sails up, his little two-stroke out-board blowing blue smoke. Wylie himself was at the tiller, his back toward Zimmerman, the boat noticeably heeling to star-board under the man's weight. Well, something to watch, anyway; better than the powerboats zipping around throwing their wakes in this no-wake zone in downtown Palmetto.

Zimmerman sipped his coffee and watched.

Wylie was barely making headway even downwind. There was little current in this broad stretch of the river where the Manatee opens up before spilling into the Gulf of Mexico. The water was calm, the wind maybe 10 knots.

Zimmerman's eyes drifted over to the big ketch anchored 100 yards out from the marina. A pretty boat, he thought. You could really cruise in a boat like that, go down around the keys and head for the islands.

He was daydreaming about the Bahamas when he heard the outboard stop, and then he saw Wylie stand and move to the mast. Maybe he was actually going to get the sails up today, he thought. The little boat drifted forward slowly as Wylie seemed to be straightening out his halyards, staring up at the masthead, hanging on to the mast with one hand.

A powerboat went by, too close to the little sailboat, and Zimmerman watched it rock back and forth on the wake and imagined Wylie hurling obscenities.

The mainsail started up slowly as Wylie pulled down on the halyard and fed the boltrope into the slot, but about halfway up it seemed to jam. It would help if he'd use the outboard to point the bow into the wind, Zimmerman thought. Even though he'd never seen the boat up close, he wondered how well it was maintained. It had a tired look from a distance. You can't let the halyards get frayed, he thought, or sometime you won't be able to get the sail down when you really need to. He knew, as it had happened to him once on his own boat—but only once.

Wylie was still beside the mast, now tugging at the sail. It came down a few feet, and then he was yanking the halyard again to try to get it up. About two-thirds of the way up it seemed to jam again. Wylie was jerking hard on the halyard. He ought to have a life jacket on, Zimmerman was thinking.

As the sailboat drifted down past the anchored ketch, Zimmerman lost sight of it for a bit, and his thoughts turned again to Bahamas cruising. He'd chartered in the Abacos once and had vivid memories of easy sailing and the red-striped lighthouse of Hope Town. That's the place to retire to, he thought, not Florida. Too many old people down here.

He was still gazing at the ketch when the little boat drifted back into view on the other side. The sail was still only two-thirds up, but the boat was heeled over away from him as if sailing a close reach. Then he realized he couldn't see Wylie. Was he down low in the cockpit getting a tool or something?

He reached for the binoculars he kept in a rack on the binnacle. He focused but still couldn't find Wylie, and the cockpit didn't look deep enough to hide him. Then he saw a line from the masthead pulled down at a funny angle on the far side of the boat, and the boat was listing to that side. Uh-oh.

Zimmerman stood and quickly surveyed the water, looking for a harbor patrol boat. Should he use the radio or the cell phone? There were no other sailboats in sight, and he guessed the powerboats down the river wouldn't have their radios on or wouldn't hear them above their engines. So he grabbed his cell phone and called 911 and made a report.

Then he looked around his marina for anyone with a boat that could be gotten out quickly, but on this Friday morning there was no one else about. It would take too long to untie all the lines of his own boat and motor out to see if he could help. Besides, by himself, unable to watch the water from the bow, he'd risk running over Wylie if he got too close.

Then he heard the siren of the marine police boat as it shot under the Green Bridge, moving fast toward the listing sailboat.

He watched through his binoculars as the police boat cautiously came abreast of the sailboat, two men near the bow looking down into the water as the driver angled in. As they stopped a few feet from the drifting sailboat, one man with a boathook reached out over the bow and caught the line down from the masthead that Zimmerman had noticed earlier.

He couldn't see what was happening on the other side of the sailboat, but he saw all three men bent over the police boat's gunwale. Together, the boats drifted farther down river.

After a couple minutes, two of the men moved back, still bent at the waist, seeming to struggle with something, and then he saw them pull a body up and over the gunwale. Because of the high freeboard of the police boat he couldn't see Wylie on the deck, but two of the men were crouched over him. The third moved up to the wheel, and the siren started wailing again.

One of the other men quickly stood and seemed to be fumbling with something. Zimmerman saw a flash of sunlight from a knife blade in his hand as he reached over and sawed through the halyard that had been pulling down on the masthead.

The sailboat bobbed and steadied, no longer listing, and one of the officers shoved it away with the boathook as the driver gunned the big outboards and spun the boat back the way it had come, the other two still bent low on the aft deck.

In a moment the police boat had disappeared back under the bridge, its siren already fading. Later that day Zimmerman would learn that they'd found Wylie facedown in the water, tied to the drifting boat by the halyard that had wrapped around one of his ankles. CPR hadn't been able to revive him.

Now, Zimmerman watched Wylie's sailboat continue to drift downriver, broadside to the wind, its sail still jammed two-thirds up, the cut halyard swinging loose. He hoped Wylie was okay. That was no way to go out, because of a lousy accident. A solo sailor himself, Zimmerman had thought often about being caught out in a bad storm, fighting wind and waves. A sudden unexpected northerly while crossing the Gulf Stream headed for the Bahamas, the seas rising monstrously—a battle. Go out fighting, struggling with the elements, not because of a stupid jammed sail.

The little daysailer, another man's dream, drifted out of sight down the river. He imagined it floating undisturbed out into Tampa Bay, then drifting through the barrier islands into the gulf and finally out of sight of land.

Then he found himself gazing wistfully at the big ketch at anchor. A big boat like that, he thought, would be safe in almost all conditions.

Briefly

Cape of Good Hope, South Africa, March 2010. The 36-year-old sailor, American-born, was well known at the Simon's Town yacht club where he had been a member for years. On this Saturday morning, like many others, he had gone sailing alone for the day. Early that evening his wife stopped in at the yacht club bar to ask if anyone had seen him, just about the same time that the club manager saw the man's boat moving about erratically at the mouth of the harbor and called authorities. Investigating boats found the sailboat unmanned and started a search. Hours later they found his body in the water, with no sign of a life jacket or tether. No one knew what had happened, but some club members speculated he may have been leaning over the side trying to start his outboard. The yacht club commodore later told a reporter, "'It will never happen to me' is the comment people usually say about these things."

Virginia Beach, Virginia, February 2011. At 8:00 in the morning, the Coast Guard received a call from the crew of a fishing boat near Little Creek Inlet that they had found a 40-foot sailboat adrift with its lights on and the engine running. Several response boats and a helicopter crew searched all day but found no sign of the missing sailor before they were finally forced to suspend the search. The boat's registration identified the owner as a very experienced 64-year-old sailor who had recently purchased the boat and was planning to sail it home to Australia. The search became a recovery effort for three more days, but his body was never found. There were no clues about why or how he apparently went overboard.

The Solent, UK, July 2012. A sailor in the Solent was sailing with his autopilot on when the wake of a passing boat rocked his sailboat and he fell overboard. He was not wearing a life jacket, and as he treaded water he watched his boat sailing on toward Cowes. Fortunately, someone spotted him in the water and called a rescue boat. A passing dredger also saw him and picked him up, and a few minutes later the rescue boat arrived and the sailor transferred to it. They then sped off and finally caught up with his sailboat, still sailing on about a mile away. He was reunited with his boat and promptly tethered in for the sail home.

Long Island Sound, Connecticut, May 2011. Early on a Friday morning a 34-foot sailboat was found floating empty off the coast of Long Island. The sails were up, the chartplotter was running, and the boatowner's wallet and glasses were in the cabin. The owner's wife reported that he had left the marina alone the previous afternoon. The water temperature was around 62°F. The sailor's body was found floating later that afternoon, with no clue about how he ended up in the water.

Chesapeake Bay, Maryland, November 2007. A sailboat with Maryland registration was found banging against a piling of the Chesapeake Bay Bridge with no one aboard. The motor was off, the mainsail was down, and the jib was up but unsecured. There were no indications of what had happened. A search was mounted but eventually called off. Four days later the body of the boat's owner was discovered washed up on shore, not wearing a life jacket.

Intracoastal Waterway, St. Johns County, Florida, February 2009. The 69-year-old sailor was last seen leaving a boat ramp at four in the afternoon. The next morning his boat was found drifting, unoccupied, in the ICW. Later that day, his body was recovered from shallow water within 50 yards of the boat. It was not clear how he had fallen overboard.

CHAPTER 11

Can Your Crew
Save You?

*M*any sailors take special precautions when sailing solo, knowing they have only themselves to depend on if something goes wrong. Many of these same sailors, however, are more relaxed and less conscientious when sailing with others, perhaps lulled by an unconscious assumption of "safety in numbers." But there are also some old salts who say that whenever you're on a boat—regardless of how many crew are on board—you should act as if you're alone, because maybe you will be.

Saturday on Lake Arthur

I told him that morning it was supposed to rain in the afternoon, but he just laughed and said something about how they always said it was going to rain when he wanted to go sailing. Besides, he said, it's just the lake, so no big deal if we have to duck in somewhere for a while, sit it out until it stops, go down in the cabin. But what about lightning, I asked. They said maybe a thunderstorm. Won't the mast attract lightning? But he just laughed like he always did.

The forecasters didn't say anything about wind. I didn't think about how windy it can get in a thunderstorm.

He was happy he'd gotten that spot at the marina so he could keep the boat on the trailer and not have to pull it back and forth like last year. And the mast didn't have to come down. It's not a big boat, just 20-something feet, but the mast is heavier than you'd think. Used to be I'd just sit and read a book while he'd wrestle it up and then back down again later before driving home.

I don't know what I'm going to do with that boat.

So I was expecting rain and put on my old tennis shoes and had my raincoat rolled up in a bag. I made us a picnic lunch and was imagining us eating in one of those pavilions they have in the park there with picnic tables and all, watching the rain fall outside. I mean, I was hoping the rain would start before we went out so we wouldn't get all wet out on the lake.

Of course it didn't. The sun was out, and mid-May already felt like July, humid like that. Hardly any wind at all, we were sweating before we even got the boat down the ramp and the truck parked again, but then it was cooler on the water.

He was grinning once we were floating, for all the world a happy man; he loved that boat. Made him act like a kid, like way back when we'd go canoeing when we were dating. A big old kid. Did I say we'd had our thirty-seventh anniversary just the week before?

So we went drifting on down the lake from the launching ramp, the breeze hardly even keeping the bugs off, but he didn't want to start that little motor to go any faster. Said he liked the quiet, so I just smiled and decided to keep quiet myself too. The sails made little flapping sounds from time to time, but other than that there was only the sound of us slapping mosquitoes and sometimes those tiny little flies. Just drifting along. We ate lunch after a while, about the time we got over to the eastern part of the lake where there aren't any roads or people. It's pretty over there early in the summer before it gets hazy, the trees fresh green on those hills all around, the water cold and clear, and if you're lucky there are no other boats roaring around. We were lucky that day— well, I mean we didn't have motorboats all around us in that part of the lake. Ordinarily that meant you were lucky.

There was only one boat that I could see, a sailboat way back the other way, back where that sailing club is. I went down there one day when he was at work to see if they gave sailing lessons. I thought I should learn something more about the boat, you know, so I could be more helpful, enjoy it more. They did have classes too, but only on Saturdays, and I'd never have been able to explain that to him. I mean, he always said he'd teach me himself, but he never did. Whenever I asked what this rope did or what that thing over there was, he'd just laugh and say I shouldn't worry about it. Just do what I ask you, he'd say, and you'll catch on by osmosis. That's what he'd say. But that osmosis never seemed to work.

So there was just that one boat and us out on the water on the east end when I saw the clouds blowing in from the west, coming in low and dark over the horizon like they had something to say. I asked him if he was going to start up the motor now and get us back before the storm, but he just cocked his head and stared at the clouds like he was looking for a secret message. Then he laughed. He always had a big laugh. I think we're about to have us a good sail now, he said.

I miss his laugh. I think that was the last time I heard it, and it sticks in my ears sometimes so I can't think about anything else.

The wind hit us almost immediately, coming from the direction of those clouds rolling in, even though they still seemed miles off. He pulled the ropes to tighten up the sails as he turned the boat back that way, and the boat leaned way over. It started blowing pretty hard then, and we just zoomed along over the water, headed for the north shore. There wasn't a beach or anything over there that I could see, just trees and rocks down to the water, but I was hoping anyway that maybe he'd just run the boat up on shore. But he didn't, he turned pretty soon in that way that you have to scoot real quick to the other side of the boat so it doesn't turn over. Then whoosh back out toward the middle of the lake, leaning over even more.

I heard him shout something about doing that turn again, so I was getting ready to slide over to the other side and trying to hang on to the picnic basket, which I should've put down below earlier. The boat was really leaning and I was kind of scared, which is probably why I was holding on so tight. I've thought about that since and decided that must be it. So he made the turn and slid over himself as the boat went over the other way real fast and there was water coming in over the side. The boat leaned way over then, and I wasn't looking at him, and then he fell out. I don't know what I was looking at, maybe my own hands trying to hold on. All that water swirling around so fast, and me sitting in it up to my waist, and to this day I don't know if I was off the boat too or if there was just that much water in the boat. Somehow I just managed to hold on. I do remember seeing the picnic basket spill out into the water; why would I remember that?

He was shouting my name. The boat had bobbed up and wasn't leaning over much now, but there was a lot of water in it. The sails were loose and flapping like crazy in the wind, so loud I couldn't hear him well at first, and then I heard him calling my name. I saw him in the water. He was a little ways off trying to swim back to the boat, but the wind was blowing the boat away faster than he could swim. Come get me, he kept shouting, and I looked at the sails flapping like devils and ropes slinging around in the wind. I grabbed the tiller thing and pushed it one way, then the other, but it didn't make any difference. Come get me—why would he yell that? I've thought about that a lot. Why didn't he yell something like throw me a life jacket? I could have done that, I could have slid through down below where he kept them and thrown one out in the water where maybe he could've swum to it. Maybe it wouldn't have blown away like the boat did. Maybe it might have kept him warmer too, since the water was so cold.

But he didn't, and I didn't think of it. I was looking at the flapping sails and trying to figure out what rope to pull when I didn't hear him calling anymore. I looked for him but couldn't see him in the water anywhere.

Then the thunderstorm hit, and the rain was so hard you couldn't see anything anywhere. The lightning was still a long way away over the hills, something I remember now even though I wasn't worried about it right then. But I don't remember much else about sitting there in the pouring rain except noticing the wind had mysteriously stopped. It was maybe 30 minutes of not thinking much at all, kind of a numbing cold, just staring at that gray water being pounded by the rain. I never even thought of looking for my raincoat. All I remember is staring at the water waiting for his arm to reach up over the side of the boat and him asking for a hand up.

Sometime after the rain stopped a couple of men came by in a little motorboat. They went around a while in big circles looking for him and then offered to tow me in. They hooked up a rope and told me to get in with them, but I said I'd just stay in the sailboat.

That would've made him laugh, I know, me choosing to stay in the wet sailboat, water up to my knees, instead of taking the dry ride. I don't know, maybe I'll keep the boat. Maybe someday I'll learn how to sail it. Maybe he'd want me to.

Wednesday Evening Club Race

When Jack and "the Boys" showed up at the club in their sports-boat for a Wednesday evening race, things were always lively. Technically, their 1720 sailboat was a keelboat and could participate in the keelboat handicap race, but a couple of the other skippers didn't much like it. With a breeze that boat could do over 20 knots, zipping around the course four times as fast as most of the real keelboat cruisers. Even the handicapping couldn't keep it from winning. Jack and the Boys had personality too. Youngish, mostly in their thirties, they partied hard in the clubhouse after races.

Tonight the wind was forecast at Force 5 to 6, and outside the harbor breakwater the Solent was sure to be kicking up. It often made for dramatic racing.

Jack had brought along an extra racer today, making a crew of six on the 8-meter boat. The other four were regular crew who had gone in with him earlier in the year to buy the 1720. They all loved its speed. With its deep bulb for ballast on a strut-like thin keel, it was a fast planing boat, like a miniature Open 50 designed for world-girdling speed races. It had a tall mast with big sails, an open transom, a long cockpit with low freeboard, and a flat foredeck for crew working the asymmetrical spinnaker. At high speeds you had to move fast to change sails or tack round a mark. All the Boys would stay pretty busy while Jack commanded the helm. He was far more experienced at racing and sailing generally than the rest of them.

This evening there were only seven boats on the line; the other six were all larger cruiser-racers with hull speeds of 7 to 8 knots. Jack was hoping for a twice-around course for the sheer fun of getting to blow by the other boats on his second lap before they finished their first.

The team had only a short time to practice before the race. They motored off the dock and then stowed the little outboard, required by the keelboat race rules, low in the cubby beside the mast step. They had just enough time to rehearse putting the spinnaker up and down once. For weeks they'd talked about doing a full practice some weekend—to let other crew try the helm, to practice a man-overboard drill and other maneuvers—but they hadn't found a time yet when everyone could make it.

Jack and the Boys. Their matching shirts were hidden under the bright colors of their waterproofs. This boat gave a wild, wet ride. As usual Jack was not wearing a life jacket, which he said slowed him down on the helm. One other crew had forgotten his in his car, but the other four wore theirs.

Today's wind let them fly the asymmetrical at the start, and within a minute they'd left the other boats behind. Out past the harbor breakwater the waves were much larger in open water, and the 1720 was flying off crests and smashing over the waves ahead. They were all grinning like kids as Jack shouted commands to the trimmers and sail handlers.

Then they came off a wave and the bowsprit pole suddenly snapped and the spinnaker flogged. Jack headed up to ease the strain, and the crew worked to get the sail down and out of the water. "Should we keep racing?" he shouted over the ruckus to the crew on the foredeck. "Just main and jib?" Everyone nodded as they bundled up the spinnaker.

Not waiting for the jib, Jack turned to get back in the race. They needed to jibe to get back toward the first mark, but in his hurry he turned too soon before the boat had gotten up enough speed and they stalled. The crew weight was poorly distributed since the others were still tending to the sails rather than stabilizing the boat for speed.

Jack gave a shout and put the helm over again. After a moment's delay the boat abruptly jibed and heeled sharply to port before Jack could reposition himself or grab on to something, and he fell overboard.

Most of the crew were still forward, but the boat's sudden motion made them look up, and they saw Jack go overboard. "Hey!" he was shouting. "Turn the boat around!"

Jack's friend, the guest crew who had never sailed the boat before, was closest to the helm and hurried to grab the tiller. The boat was being tossed about as he brought it over, but then they were caught in irons facing the wind. Already the boat had been blown some distance away from where Jack was struggling in the waves.

One of the crew was pushing out the boom to get the boat to fall off and make some speed for steering. Two others on the bow, still trying to secure the spinnaker before it was blown off the deck, saw another boat in the race catching up nearby. They shouted to it, pointing to Jack in the water.

The skipper of the cruising sailboat understood the situation immediately and started his diesel to power into the wind in Jack's direction. The sails were left to flog as his crew watched for the man in the water. The skipper grabbed the VHF microphone and called the Coastguard, gave his position, and asked for a lifeboat. He waited for his crew to shout and point out Jack's location, but they were silent, watching the water intently. After a few minutes he realized they must have missed him and gone too far, so he turned back for another pass.

On the 1720 another crew had taken over the helm and was tacking back to where they thought Jack was in the water.

Two men watched from the bow. At last one of them spotted Jack about 10 meters away floating facedown. He shouted and pointed and then without hesitation dived in and started swimming for Jack. But as he was wearing a life jacket, he could only swim slowly.

The helmsman quickly tacked, and in moments the boat moved past the swimming crew and reached Jack's position. Two crew reached overboard and grabbed Jack's jacket. But in their hurry they hadn't thought to release the sheets, and the boat was still moving too fast for them to hold on. One felt the jacket pull away from his fingers, and the other—the crew who had left his life jacket in the car—tumbled into the water still holding on to Jack. As the boat moved on past them he grabbed a line trailing behind but could not keep hold of it.

The first 1720 crew who had jumped in wearing a life jacket now reached Jack and took him from the other one who had no life jacket. The 1720 was still moving off as the three left on board started maneuvers to get the boat turned around and back to the three in the water.

The cruising sailboat was now returning to the area, its skipper having seen the others enter the water and reach Jack. As he approached, slowing, the man without a life jacket swam over and was able to clamber up the meter of freeboard with the help of the crew aboard. Then the boat maneuvered through the waves to the other two.

They lowered a line, and the crew in the water tied it around Jack's chest under his armpits, but they weren't able to pull him all the way up. He was unresponsive, and they couldn't tell if he was breathing. With their mainsail still up and flogging they couldn't control the boom well enough to use it for leverage to hoist Jack up. The skipper had just called for his crew to get the sails down when he saw the lifeboat racing toward them. In less than a minute the lifeboat crew had Jack on board and were stripping off his jacket to start CPR. The other crew was helped out of the water and on board the cruising sailboat.

It had been only 10 minutes since Jack had fallen in, but the water was cold and the waves and spray would have made it difficult to breathe while attempting to tread water.

Soon a Coastguard helicopter arrived and winched Jack from the lifeboat and flew back to town.

He was pronounced dead at the hospital.

None of them was ever able to explain how everything happened so fast and how what should have been a simple matter of getting back to him in the water went so wrong.

Four Miles off Hyannis

"You'd better go out today with your granddad," Ethan's grandmother had said that morning. "Frankly, at his age, we can't know how many more years he'll be sailing."

Ethan looked out the window at the heavy clouds boiling past. "You think he still wants to go in weather like this?"

"He knows you're leaving for college in a couple days. Besides, it pretty much takes a hurricane to keep him in port."

So they went sailing, Ethan, age 19, with his maternal grandfather, age 77. It felt chilly in the wind for August on the cape but at least it wasn't raining. And Ethan really did want to spend time with Grandpa. He was an interesting man and told great stories, which were even better when the women weren't around. As for the sailing, well, Ethan didn't know much about that part; in fact, he'd never sailed before. He'd grown up in the Midwest far from any sizable body of water and had mostly visited his grandparents in Massachusetts over the winter holidays.

It sure was a beautiful boat, though. As they stowed their things on board and got underway, Grandpa was explaining that it was a schooner, a small one at 30 feet, but the real thing. He explained about the gaffs and masts and Ethan nodded, not really understanding. Well, he was only along for the ride, and was looking forward to Grandpa's promise that they'd have a traditional taste of rum when they got back to harbor.

It started raining just after they got the sails up—Ethan had helped by pulling on the ropes Grandpa pointed to—but Grandpa only gestured at the hatch and told him to fetch their oilskins.

"Huh?"

"Rain gear, son. Used to be made of canvas or leather with a skin of oil for waterproofing. Get it, oilskins?"

While he was down below Ethan checked his cell phone quickly for any texts that might have come in. Nothing. At least he had a signal.

When he came back up with the rain gear he noticed the wind had picked up. He looked around at the waves and saw only one other boat, a small powerboat that was streaking back in the direction of shore. They quickly put on their rain jackets and their life jackets on over them.

On they sailed, Grandpa holding the spokes of the wooden wheel and occasionally asking Ethan to pull in or let out this line or that. Except for the rain in his eyes he was starting to enjoy it. The sailboat leaned over to one side, and he sat in the cockpit on the high side, watching the curling waves past Grandpa. The boat was rolling right along.

Usually a taciturn man, Grandpa now kept up a steady stream of talk, mostly about other sailing voyages he'd taken. Clearly a happy man when sailing, showing no signs of his age, his hands moved the wheel as he watched the waves, oblivious to the rain on his face. He wore an old black watch cap low over his eyes, the hood of his raincoat like a monk's cowl.

"Ready to try steering for a while?" he said after a time.

"Sure, Grandpa."

"Come around over here. I'll stand behind you to guide you."

Ethan stood and moved across the canting cockpit to join Grandpa at the wheel. When he had it in his grip, Grandpa let go and stepped back. Just then a bigger wave hit the boat, and in the sudden lurch Grandpa lost his balance and tilted back, falling, and was pitched backward off the boat.

In horror Ethan let go of the wheel and turned around.

Grandpa was in the water some 20 feet back already. "Throw me the cushion!" he shouted.

Ethan grabbed the orange cushion his grandfather had been sitting on and threw it as far as he could back into the water. But he couldn't see where it landed, and then he couldn't even see his grandfather. The waves looked big and confused, and the pelting rain made it hard to see. Oh shit, Ethan thought, oh shit, oh shit, now what do I do?

The wheel was moving erratically, and the boat seemed to be turning broadside to the waves, bouncing and slamming more. He took the wheel and held it, then looked back into the turmoil of water behind the boat. He had to get back, but already he was confused. Where was Grandpa? Where was he? Which way was land? The sky was dark gray and the air was full of water; it looked the same in all directions. Then he thought, the waves. He remembered the angle they'd been coming from before, sort of from the front left side, so Grandpa must be—he looked, thought about it— back that way.

He slowly turned the wheel to the right, watching to see what would happen. He couldn't tell if the boat was turning, nothing seemed to change, but then the boat stopped leaning quite as much. He watched the waves while turning some more. Now the waves were coming from behind him, and they looked huge, scary, higher than his head, but on each wave the back of the boat rose and the wave passed under.

Maybe now he was going the right way back. He moved the wheel back to center and held it tight, leaning out to one side, trying to watch the water ahead.

There was a sudden pause, a weird lull, and he glanced up from the water as the huge sail above him came swinging back fast. He instinctively ducked as the boom passed overhead, and the sail shot out to the other side with a huge roar and a sharp crack and jolt that almost knocked him off his feet. Turn, turn! he thought, but which way?

It was like being on another planet. He didn't have the slightest idea what to do, or where his grandfather was, or how to get to him. He could only hope his grandfather was okay, floating in the water in his life jacket, waiting for Ethan to come and get him.

He's going to die, he thought then, and it's my fault and I'll have to tell Grandma.

The wind and rain tore at him. Everything was terrifying. It felt like the boat would sink any minute.

Then he remembered his cell phone. Shit! Why hadn't he thought of it before?

He didn't dare get it wet in the drenching rain, so he let go of the wheel and dashed for the hatch to get below. Just as he ducked in he saw the sail swinging across again and braced himself for the shock when it hit. Then he punched in 911 and waited an eternity for a connection.

He shouted it all quickly to the dispatcher in case the phone died, and the woman seemed to understand. "Keep your phone on," she told him. "The GPS will give us your location. We're coming."

For a moment he felt relief at knowing someone else was in charge now. Then he had a vision of Grandpa in the water, the waves throwing him around, all alone in the ocean; they'd never find him. He'd waited too long to call; they might know where *he* was, but what about Grandpa?

He rushed back up on deck to keep watching the water.

The waves were more to the right side now, still from behind, and he realized the problem with the sail happened when the waves came directly from behind. So he started steering in a way to keep the waves in the same place. But he had no idea whether Grandpa was ahead of him or behind or somewhere else. He wanted to get back on the phone to ask if they were coming, but then he might run down the battery and maybe they still needed the GPS signal.

There was nothing he could do. He should've asked Grandpa how to sail the boat, what you're supposed to do with the sails and all those ropes to make it go the way you wanted. He should've paid more attention. But even if he knew, he thought, he still didn't know which way to go.

That was the worst of it: there was nothing he could do except watch the water and try to keep the boat from sinking. And think about how he was going to explain this to Grandma—and later, to Mom.

The rain fell and gusts of wind shook the old schooner, but only a little water was sloshing over the sides and somehow it kept moving.

After a while he thought to look at his watch and was surprised to see almost an hour had passed. He was steering listlessly now, mechanically, just watching the endless passage of endless waves. It wasn't raining quite as hard now. But still he saw nothing in any direction. For the first time he thought that he too might die.

He found himself staring at the compass mounted in front of the wheel. Shit! Why hadn't he thought of it before? He could've figured out which way the boat pointed, which way to Grandpa, but now after an hour it was too late. What a fool he was. He stared at the thing. It looked like the boat was pointed north. It took long seconds before he could visualize a map of the cape and their starting point in Hyannis Harbor. North—that meant he was sailing back toward land.

He was in no hurry to get there and have to tell everyone what had happened.

Holding the wheel tight, he carefully stood to look ahead past the bow. In the distance he saw a smudge that might be land.

Then he saw another boat speeding toward him from one side. He waved. The boat came on, and soon he saw the slash of orange that meant the Coast Guard.

The boat came in closer, and a man was shouting at him through a megaphone. "Drop your sails!" he said. "We'll come get you!"

Ethan gestured futilely.

The man ducked inside, then reemerged as the boat started working toward him slowly. Other men on deck readied ropes and hung big orange balls over the side.

As the boats touched, two men jumped over quickly. One went forward with a coil of rope, the other came back to Ethan. "I'll help you over to our vessel," he said. "Let me get this line around you, then we'll get the sails down."

"But—"

The man looked up. "Oh yes, they found him with the helicopter. He was cold but alive."

Ethan started to cry.

The crew got the sails down, and they took the schooner in tow after getting Ethan across to the cutter. They took him inside where the woman on the helm was talking on the radio. She held up a finger for him to wait. Ethan couldn't make out what the radio was saying. Then she turned to him. "They just heard from the hospital. He's going to be okay."

Ethan slumped into a seat.

Someone else came over. "The helicopter crew didn't think they'd find him," he said. "With all the rain, and fog moving in, they couldn't see anything. Then they thought they saw a buoy or something, and they went lower and there he was, waving this bright orange cushion over his head. He's a lucky man, your grandfather. They got him up in a minute and flew straight to the hospital."

Ethan couldn't speak. After a few minutes he was calmer and asked if he could call his grandmother.

"She already knows he's okay. She's probably on her way to the hospital right now."

"Can we get a message to my grandfather then?" Ethan asked. He looked back out the window to where the schooner was riding proud through the waves. "Tell him his boat's okay, that I didn't sink it or anything."

Briefly

Columbia River, Washington, October 2010. An experienced sailor reputed to be a good swimmer, age 46, was sailing in the

5-mile-wide stretch of the river east of Astoria with his two children when a strong gust heeled the boat and he toppled overboard. He was not wearing a life jacket. The children saw him in the water, but the 18-year-old who took the wheel was not able to get the boat back to him before he went under in the cold water. The kids radioed for help, but the responding Coast Guard boat and helicopter were not able to find him before having to abandon the search late that night.

Lake Erie, Ohio, July 2010. A crew of three were sailing in Lake Erie not far from Port Clinton when they decided to use the auxiliary inboard engine to return to port because conditions had gotten rough. As the boat bounced around in the choppy water, one of the jibsheets slipped overboard and fouled the prop, stalling the engine. The owner removed his life jacket and entered the water, intending to cut the line from the prop, but the waves pulled him away from the boat and the wind blew the boat away from him faster than he could swim to it. The other two were unable to get back upwind to him in time, and he went under. Searchers were unable to recover his body.

Narragansett Bay, Rhode Island, 2008. A man and his wife were just beginning a day's sail on the bay. While motoring out to open water, the man stood to raise the mainsail, directing his wife to turn into the wind. The boat accidentally jibed, however, and the boom swung across fast and struck him in the head, knocking him overboard. She was unable to rescue him. His body was recovered 3 days later.

San Diego Bay, California, July 2012. The owner of a 36-foot sailboat was taking two guests out for an afternoon sail on the bay. One of the jibsheets got hung up on a foredeck cleat, and the owner turned the wheel over to one of the guests and went forward to clear it. As the boat bounced on a wave he lost his balance and fell overboard, not wearing a life jacket. The two guests had no sailing experience and had no idea of how to turn the boat back to reach him, but they were able to radio for help. Later, harbor police recovered his body.

CHAPTER 12

What Could Possibly Go Wrong?

T*he stories in previous chapters have illustrated the many things that can go wrong when sailing, often with disastrous results. A key issue in those stories, as in almost all sailing and boating disasters, is that the people involved were not expecting trouble. What could possibly go wrong on a fine day like any other? But in virtually all cases, lives could have been saved if only the sailors had really thought about that question. Lots of things can go wrong, and regularly do. What happens next may depend on luck, as the rescues in some of these stories demonstrate, or on preparations made or actions taken in advance. When you do ask and honestly answer the question of what can possibly go wrong, you're much more likely to live to tell the tale. Accidents still happen, but when they do, as we see in the following four brief narratives, the sailors who prepare for them, who frequently think in "what if" terms, are sailors who live to sail again.*

Capsize in Puget Sound

Blake didn't consider himself a very experienced sailor. He'd learned to sail only a year ago after moving to the Tala Point area north of Seattle. He first sailed with a man he worked with who sailed a Catalina 30 on the sound. Blake loved it immediately: the wind and water, the beauty of the islands, the sheer joy of the boat cutting a line through waves, the music of water along the hull—the whole experience.

Unfortunately, his friend insisted on doing everything himself, so Blake didn't feel he learned much. Rather than wait to be invited out again on the boat, he signed up for sailing lessons at a nearby yacht club. They told him that at age 40 he'd be mostly in with kids and teenagers, but he didn't mind. He just wanted to sail.

The sailing class used 14-foot Hunter daysailers, two crew to a boat, with an open deck and long cockpit, but they felt like "real" sailboats with a jib, a mainsail, and sail controls, including a vang and leech tension lines. He learned how to position his weight, use the centerboard to advantage, and avoid overtrimming the sails. He learned a lot and loved it all.

And now he had his own sailboat, a chubby 15-footer with a tiny cuddy cabin, beamier and heavier and slower than the club boats, a little old and a little beat up—and it was great. He had bought it in the fall and found it hard to wait for spring. Through the winter he read sailing books and magazines and made frequent visits to his local chandlery, marveling at all the boat gear. Marveling too at what it cost to own a boat! But he was determined to do it right, and he chose his gear after researching options online. He hadn't much liked the life jackets at the sailing school, so he bought an inflatable PFD that felt good and had a built-in harness. He bought new docklines because the old ones were frayed. He inspected the rigging closely for any weak points. He discovered the flares on the boat had expired and bought new ones. All the while he was imagining himself out in the sound, sailing his own boat among the San Juan Islands, camping aboard, exploring hidden coves. He was reading classic sailing narratives too, which taught him about things that sometimes happened out there. He bought a tether for his harness. He bought a submersible handheld VHF.

Friends visiting his small apartment surveyed the heap of gear and joked he was getting obsessed.

Then, finally, spring arrived, and with it, sailing! It was all as good as he'd imagined it.

On his fourth weekend he made a small mistake while out sailing alone, turning without first releasing the mainsheet from the jam cleat, and a gust knocked over the boat. The rail went under, the cockpit filled, the mast went down, and the boat kept rolling.

Blake jumped and was clear when the boat turned turtle, his PFD inflating with a bang and its bladder filling around his neck as it ripped open the Velcro cover. He floated easily, staring at his upside-down boat, imagining his precious gear tumbling out to the bottom below.

There was nothing he could hold on to except the rudder, and he saw immediately that the heavy centerboard had fallen back into its trunk. He pulled himself as high on the hull as he could, but no part of the board emerged from the hull, and he assumed there was no way he could get the board extended again to try to right the boat, as he'd learned in the smaller sailboats at the club. He was screwed. And the water was cold.

He pulled himself up again and looked all around, but there were no boats close enough to see him. So he held on to the rudder with one hand while with the other he reached down and unclipped the VHF radio from his belt. Thank god he'd bought one that was submersible.

He switched it on, was thrilled to see the screen light up, and called the Coast Guard on channel 16. They answered immediately. He felt sheepish as he explained what had happened, but they took his information and said help would be on the way and to keep the radio on.

He was surprised by how quickly the helicopter arrived. It hovered overhead, and the crew called him on the radio to see how he was doing. He said he was cold but okay and was not having any problem holding on to the boat.

The helicopter remained nearby until a Coast Guard cutter appeared not long after. They had him on board in a minute, and then one of their crew in a wet suit went into the water with a line and attached it to the sailboat so that they could pull the boat over and back upright.

While they worked with his boat, Blake kept apologizing for causing all this trouble, but the crew assured him that's what they were there for. They asked if he wanted them to tow the boat back, but everything looked fine when they'd pumped it out and checked the rigging.

"Can I sail it back?" he asked.

"Sure," a guardsman said. "That's what you came out for, right, the sailing?"

He had removed the uncomfortably inflated PFD and switched to his spare life jacket, and now made a final check of his gear and the sails.

"Just keep that life jacket on, right?" called one of the crew. Too often they'd had to do recoveries when boaters didn't.

Capsize in Lake Huron

When Jackson planned his move to Michigan from North Carolina, he looked for an affordable place to live as close as possible to Lake Huron. Over the last couple of summers he'd sailed his Hobie catamaran as often as he could, and he planned to keep on sailing on the Great Lakes. He and his wife towed the boat all the way behind his pickup.

Both the air and water were cooler on Lake Huron than Pamlico Sound, but otherwise it felt just as good to be out on the water, flying hull when the wind was good. Soon he had his new Michigan friends joining him on the weekends when the weather was good. His wife enjoyed other pursuits but seldom complained about how he spent his Saturdays.

On this Saturday afternoon, two of his friends had come along and they'd had a blast. The wind was good and his crew, who had sailed with him before, knew what to do. Even better, it was a warm day for early October with good wind. His only regret was that the others had to leave by four o'clock, so he sailed them both back to the beach. The day was so perfect for sailing, though, that he couldn't just stop so early. So he let them off and headed back out into the lake for another hour or two of sailing, as if he could bank the experience for the coming winter.

He shot off straight out into the lake to where the wind was stronger and steadier. A couple of miles out, the wind was perfect and he turned slightly, onto a beam reach. The windward hull rose high from the water, and he felt the thrill of riding the fine line of control, hiked out on the high hull, the boat like a nimble extension of his own body.

Until he relaxed just a little too much and responded too slowly to a gust and the cat went over.

The cold water was shocking—this was the first time he'd flipped since North Carolina—but he floated well in his life jacket and wasn't worried. He'd righted the cat several times back in North Carolina, and the waves weren't high enough to be troublesome, so he wasn't worried.

Then he realized the mast had gone much deeper in the water and the position of the hulls was different than in the past. He stared at the boat, trying to make sense of what he was seeing. The angle of the hulls suggested the mast was some 45 degrees into the water. That made no sense. He'd made his own masthead float, and it had always had enough buoyancy to keep the masthead at or near the surface. At that angle it was easy to stand on the lower hull, grab the line tied to the other hull, and lean back to pull the boat back upright. But now with the mast far underwater, the hulls were positioned differently. He climbed up on the bottom hull and reached forward to the upper hull, but it was too far over and the lifting line was too short to let him pull back with enough force to pivot the boat back up.

He tried over and over, but he simply had no leverage. What had happened?

Then he remembered something from his college physics class: salt water is denser than fresh water and provides more buoyancy. The masthead float that had worked in North Carolina didn't work as well here; it was just too small for the lesser buoyancy of fresh water.

He looked around but saw no boats nearby. It was after five o'clock now, and the few distant boats were headed back toward marinas. Dark came early in October. Already the air was cooling, and he shivered in his wet T-shirt and shorts.

Surely, he thought, someone will see me standing on the capsized hull. But as the sun sank, no boat had come close enough.

There was nothing to do but wait. He hoped his wife remembered that he'd said he would be home by six, and would call someone for help.

But once it was full dark, he started thinking the odds were slim they'd find him even if they came looking. It's a huge lake, and he could've been anywhere. He tried to remember the forecast and how cold it would get. Carefully balancing on the hull, he stripped off his T-shirt and tried to wring it dry, but he was shivering now with or without the shirt. That worried him; he'd heard about hypothermia and how you eventually lost muscle control. If he fell back into the cold water, he didn't think he'd last long, maybe not until daylight.

He watched the lights on the distant shore, the running lights of occasional faraway boats, the tiny light of a passing jet overhead. He couldn't stop shivering, and sometimes his arms shook hard. He was trying to think what to do, but thinking was arduous. He'd been standing for hours, sometimes balanced, sometimes leaning forward uncomfortably to hold the other hull, and all he wanted was to sit, but he worried about having his legs in the cold water.

Then he saw another airplane, lower this time, between him and the shore, moving slowly left to right. Then it moved farther away. Suddenly there was a burst of light below it, a bright blast of light below the plane, which drifted slowly down and went out as it reached the water.

The plane turned and went back, right to left, closer now. It turned again a couple of minutes later. Then there was another blast of light, and he realized it was dropping flares. This one was close enough to shine white on his skin, and he began waving his arms.

After a moment the plane turned, banking, flew directly over-head, and dropped another flare. He was shouting now, waving frantically.

The plane went on and banked into a slow turn back. Had they seen him?

Then he heard a boat engine that gradually grew louder, and at last he saw paired red and green lights becoming larger as the boat approached.

The rescue boat crew found him with their spotlight and within a couple minutes had eased up to the capsized catamaran and helped him aboard. His wife had called 911 at 6:15, he learned, and they'd been searching with boats closer to shore for hours, doubting he'd be out so far. Then they'd called in the Hercules search-and-rescue plane. "Good thing your wife called fast," they told him. "There's a lot of water out here."

Sinking in the Georgia Strait

Sampson was tired. He'd planned to be back at the marina in Van-couver, British Columbia, by midnight, but here it was already after 1 A.M. and he was still a few miles north of Entrance Island, miles offshore in the middle of the Georgia Strait. The wind had all but died at sunset, and he wasn't sure he had enough diesel left after days of cruising to make it all the way in under power. So he jogged along slowly in the 8-knot breeze.

Not that he was in any real hurry. He was just sleepy. He'd turned off the autopilot to steer his 36-foot sloop by hand, which helped him stay alert. But time had just crawled by while the boat made barely 2 knots.

He caught himself yawning again and thought he'd better have a cup of coffee. He stood in the cockpit and checked all around for any ships, then reset the autopilot, unclipped his tether from the U-bolt when he approached the companionway, and went down the steps.

And found himself standing in 20 centimeters of water.

Instantly he was wide awake. He flipped on several cabin lights and grabbed a flashlight. It had to be a through-hull fitting, he reasoned, he hadn't been going fast enough to punch a hole in the hull if he'd hit anything. A hose might have come off or burst, or perhaps a seacock had broken. He had wooden plugs wired by each of the through-hulls, and he quickly grabbed the mallet from where it hung near the engine compartment door. Just find the one leaking, he thought. He knew what to do.

He started with the engine compartment, which opened behind the companionway steps. There was the cooling-water intake, two hose outlets from the cockpit drains, and of course the stuffing box and shaft gland. And far back, the rudderpost.

He shone the light in. Already the water was over the bottom of the engine, sloshing back and forth, but he saw nothing that looked like an inflow. He felt in the water and found the cooling-water intake hose at the seacock; it seemed fine. The cockpit drain hoses were farther back, but there was no upwelling of water near either that indicated a leak. He couldn't see the shaft gland or rudderpost from here, but they were less likely sources. He'd have to climb back in the quarter berth and remove the side panel to check them, and that would take a minute or two. So he pulled his head and shoulders out, noticing that the batteries on one side were already halfway immersed, and quickly moved to the head.

Beneath the sink were the through-hulls for the sink drain and the intake for the head. It was hard to reach his head in and shine the flashlight through the small opening at the same time, so he felt around in the water. He cursed himself for not putting on his headlamp instead of grabbing the flashlight, but the water was still rising and he didn't want to go back for it now.

He couldn't feel any water flow, so he pulled back out and went to the galley. Under the sink were another drain through-hull and an intake for the sink's saltwater foot pump. He pulled the cabinet door open and removed a stack of pans and pots, feeling deep into the watery space, running his hands over the hoses down to the seacocks. Nothing felt wrong.

He yanked up the floorboard over the bilge pump and with his hand felt the vibration of the little motor. No sign of water rushing in from the through-hull for the speed transducer.

Then he realized he'd been assuming the leak was at or near a through-hull fitting, when it might be in any of the hoses a half a meter back from the fitting, anywhere below the waterline. He stood, intending to go back to the engine compartment, but the cabin lights suddenly went out. He paused a moment, feeling the boat's motion, and knew the boat was sliding off course now that the autopilot had failed. The batteries had shorted out in the water, so he wouldn't be able to start the engine now either.

He sloshed back to the engine compartment and shone the light inside again. The water was much deeper now, completely over the batteries, and he knew he didn't have much time. If the water had risen so fast with the bilge pump running, it would be even faster now, and much faster than he could pump it out manually. He had to find the leak soon. He shone the light everywhere, hoping to see a bubbling or upwelling of water or a current, anything to indicate where it was getting in. But he saw nothing, just deepening water.

Did he have time to pump up the inflatable dinghy? Why hadn't he kept it inflated and just lashed it on the foredeck? Because he didn't like how it partially blocked his view forward, that's why. And the waves were often too high to tow it. No, he thought, not enough time.

He glanced once at his gear piled on the starboard quarter berth, then went back up to the cockpit.

Of course the chartplotter was dead too, as was his radio, but in his deck bag slung over the binnacle he had a backup battery-powered GPS and his handheld VHF. He turned on the GPS first and waited 2 painful minutes for it to find his location while he surveyed the water for any ships. Nothing.

When he had his longitude and latitude location, he switched on the VHF, happy to see the battery indicator said near full. Then he made a Mayday call.

Nanaimo Marine Rescue answered immediately. He gave his name and location and said the boat was sinking. They said they were launching search boats. The Canadian Coast Guard came on the radio then and said they would be underway in their fast hovercraft.

He repeated his location, then shone the light back down the companionway where black water was over the tops of the berths. "I'm preparing to abandon ship," he said, "but will stay with the boat unless it goes down. I have a dry suit, and the radio batteries look good."

"We're on our way," both rescue centers responded.

Getting into his dry suit was tedious work, and when he had to put down the flashlight to use both hands, it rolled into the water. It was lit for a moment deep below the surface but then went out. So much for waterproof flashlights, he thought. He made sure the submersible VHF was still clipped to the loop on the dry suit.

He started to release the halyards to drop the sails in case any boat motion was hastening the leak, but he thought they might be more visible for the searchers. He left them up but released the sheets so that they flapped listlessly.

The boat was settling deep in the water, and a wave sloshed over the rail and cockpit coaming. He scanned the water all around for lights of boats.

What happened when a boat went down? People talked about being sucked down after it, but he thought that probably only happened with big ships. On the other hand, he was concerned that at the last moment the boat might roll or pitch and snag him in the rigging. It seemed safer to be off the boat before that happened.

So he waited until it looked like the cockpit would soon flood, then unclipped the VHF and called to say the boat was about to go down and he was getting into the water. He felt in the pocket of the dry suit and told them he had a glow stick and would snap it on when he saw a rescue boat getting close. "Watch for a small green light," he said, and signed off.

He stepped off the stern into the water and breast-stroked slowly away from the boat, feeling awkward in the dry suit. He felt warm enough except for the cold water that splashed his face.

Then he stopped and floated and watched his sailboat go down. It just slipped beneath the water, still upright, until even the masthead was gone, and he felt a deep sadness for the first time. Such a mystery, the unknown fast leak. He'd never even know what it was.

He figured it was only about 15 minutes before he saw the Coast Guard hovercraft approaching, throwing up white spray in the moonlight. He snapped the green glow stick and held it as high as he could. Its light looked uselessly feeble, but he saw the hovercraft alter course a little and slow its approach. In a minute they were pulling him aboard.

Bahia Transat Disaster

Mini class 6.50-meter sailboats are very fast race boats and can be a handful to sail, especially for the singlehanded sailors of the Charente-Maritime Transat, which in 2011 ran from France to Brazil via Madeira, a 4,200-nautical mile sprint. It's a grueling race for solo sailors, who must be at the top of their game and prepared for many strenuous days alone at sea. For many, it's also a significant test of self-sufficiency. Regardless of the team support and the best work of designers and engineers, once the boats leave the dock these skippers are as much on their own as any sailor can be out on the ocean, even with satellite linkups.

French sailor Mathieu Claveau was in the middle of the Atlantic, pushing on in his small boat, catching some sleep in a period of light wind, when he was abruptly awakened by what he later described as the powerful shock of the boat striking something. He rushed on deck but saw nothing in the water nearby. Then he experienced every sailor's nightmare: he looked below and saw water gushing into his boat, already covering the cabin sole. Kneeling, he felt along the hull in his galley area and found a gaping, ragged hole so large it would be impossible to plug in time. There were no boats in sight; he was alone at sea and sinking.

But ocean races like this one have stringent safety requirements, and Claveau had an EPIRB as well as a life raft and enough emergency gear to stay alive for days if needed. He tried bailing water from the boat but realized immediately he could not keep up. He then activated his emergency beacon and started gathering his gear to abandon ship.

He had to trust that his signal would be received and help dispatched; he had no other hope. Even with a supply of food and water he couldn't expect to survive forever in a tiny life raft. The literature of sail includes many stories of sailors spilled from their life rafts by storms at sea or drifting for weeks after running out of food and water. In 1981 Steve Callahan spent 76 days in a life raft in the Atlantic in the days before satellite GPS and EPIRBs, subsisting on fish, birds, barnacles, and rainwater. He was very lucky to have survived.

As it happened, Claveau was lucky that a cargo ship was only 45 miles away when his emergency signal was received. The ship was diverted to his location and soon reached him. As instructed by the Maritime Rescue Coordination Centre, the ship stopped on his weather side to enable its crew to help him board from his life raft, along with the first-aid bag he still clutched. The entire incident, start to finish, lasted only a couple of hours.

$$\bullet\bullet\bullet--—\bullet\bullet\bullet$$

Although the rescue would have been more difficult in a storm than in the relatively calm seas, the outcome likely would still have been favorable because Claveau had the appropriate safety gear on his boat and was prepared to use it. With such gear now readily available to all, in recent years there have been very few fatalities among those who are so equipped. The days of frequent disasters during storms and other incidents at sea are rapidly receding, even as the common, everyday "little" incidents like tumbling overboard on a calm day continue to claim lives.

Most important, gear like an EPIRB is not only for well-financed racing teams or wealthy sailors. These units are now so inexpensive that every boatowner can have one, or at minimum a PLB or submersible handheld VHF radio (in areas of coverage) for coastal and even lake sailing. (These devices should always be registered by the owner to expedite the search-and-rescue procedures followed when an emergency signal is received.) And in most cases, near shore, you don't need a life raft; a good PFD will keep most sailors afloat and alive until rescue arrives as long as they also have the means to summon help.

Almost every sailor who met a tragic ending in the stories in this book could have been saved by this simple combination of equipment along with a "what if" attitude toward always being prepared.

Interview with Gary Jobson, President of U.S. Sailing

Gary Jobson, a lifelong sailor and racer, is currently president of U.S. Sailing, the governing body for the sport in the United States. A former winning tactician in the America's Cup, he has written 17 books on many aspects of sailing and is generally regarded as the premier spokesman for the sport of sailing. On March 2, 2012, he spoke to me about his attitude toward safety issues when sailing.

You've had a very long sailing career on many different types of boats and races and in all kinds of waters. Have you come close to emergency situations yourself?
I've been in several situations that involved fatalities on sailboats. During the 2002 Block Island Race, a crew on the boat I was on was hit in the head by a spinnaker pole and went over the side and drowned. It was very traumatic. Another time I was on a ship where a man fell off a lifeboat and hit his head, and he died. I was also in the [1979] Fastnet Race off England when 15 sailors died during that storm. Last year I helped put together the investigation after Olivia Constants died while sailing a 420 near Annapolis where I live [see Chapter 2]. We all know there's some risk on the water, but it's very sad and unfortunate when things like this happen.

What can be done to help sailors stay safe on the water? Is it a matter of teaching so people are more aware of what can happen?
I definitely believe in teaching safety. After the Fastnet storm in 1979, U.S. Sailing created a Safety at Sea seminar series. For our distance ocean races now it's mandatory to take one of these safety seminars at least every 5 years. They really make a difference. You go through these scenarios; like if somebody goes over the side, we go through the routine—the safe way to save the person, doing crew-overboard drills, the whole step-by-step process. The fact that you've talked about it, you know the equipment and how to use it, testing your inflatable PFD—everything. It gives you a much better chance if something happens.

It's especially important if you're new to sailing or you just bought your boat. It's worth the time to take a safety course, get some instruction, or hire a coach for a day, so you know how to operate the boat, what to do if the weather goes bad, and so on.

How should we talk about the everyday safety issues that can arise when sailing?
I think you need to strike a balance. Sailing is fun, it's accessible to everyone, and it's a great sport, good for all ages. But you need to balance that with the message you have to be careful, safety is an important issue, and we want to do it properly.

What other preparations do you advise sailors to take?
Whenever you're going sailing you need to be able to call for help; take a radio with you. Tell someone where you're going and what time you expect to get back. Sometimes it's just that simple. Then, when you're on the boat, be purposeful. Pay attention to everything. Someone's on the helm, someone's keeping a lookout, someone's paying attention to the sails—as opposed to kicking back with a beer and letting the boat sail itself. You have fewer accidents when people are paying attention to everything going on.

And common sense counts. If your dog goes overboard and you're by yourself, your first impulse may be to jump in and save the dog, but it's better to think a second and then sail over and haul the dog back on board.

What about wearing a PFD?

When I race a sailboat like an Etchells or a Laser, I always wear a PFD. I just always do it. I try to set an example. Even when I'm sailing by myself casually, I still wear a PFD. You just can't afford not to.

Anything else?

I always think it's important to try to educate people, so I think your book is going to provide a service to someone you'll never know: they're going to read it and take note and do some of these things to stay safe. So I applaud what you're doing.

mL   4/4